D1557089

By Doug Hannon

& Don Wirth

Published By

GREAT OUTDOORS PUBLISHING CO.
4747 TWENTY-EIGHTH STREET NORTH
ST. PETERSBURG, FLORIDA 33714

DEDICATION

To my wife and the great State of Florida
for the inspiration and fulfillment
of my fishing dreams.

Library of Congress Catalog Card Number: 84-73347

First Printing: December, 1984

ISBN: 0-8200-0123-6

A special thanks to Bob Cobb, Editor, *Bassmaster Magazine,* for providing the forum that made this writing partnership possible.

Printed in the United States of America

Contents

Cover Photograph: A large-mouth bass strikes a Burke "Weedbeater" lure.

Doug Hannon

DOUG HANNON is widely acknowledged as the world's leading authority on the largemouth bass, and has earned the nickname, "The Bass Professor." A former bass guide, Hannon took clients fishing only with the stipulation that one trophy fish be kept and all others released. He has probably caught and released more huge bass (fish over 14 lbs.) than any living person, and holds the astounding record of over 400 bass exceeding 10 lbs. apiece caught and released. No one knows more about the habits and mysteries of the bass, and Hannon's viewpoint has appeared in virtually every outdoor magazine. Hannon is an underwater photographer, lecturer, and author on the subject of the bass and successful bass fishing; he is also an inventor and lure designer. His conservation views led to the development of potions to aid in the successful release of bass. Hannon lives near Tampa, Florida. He holds a B.A. from Tulane University.

Don Wirth

DON WIRTH is one of the most prolific and widely-read writers on the bass fishing scene, with regular contributions appearing in Bassmaster Magazine, Pro Bass, Rooster Tales, and other publications. He first met Doug Hannon when doing a feature article about Hannon's controversial conservation stands, and has since collaborated with "The Bass Professor" on several articles for Bassmaster. Wirth has an extensive background in advertising as a copywriter, video and music producer, and creative director. He holds a B.A. in journalism from the University of Iowa and an M.A. in journalism from the University of Missouri. Wirth lives in Nashville, Tennessee. He is the author of two other books, The Adventures of Harry 'n Charlie and The Bass Boat Bible.

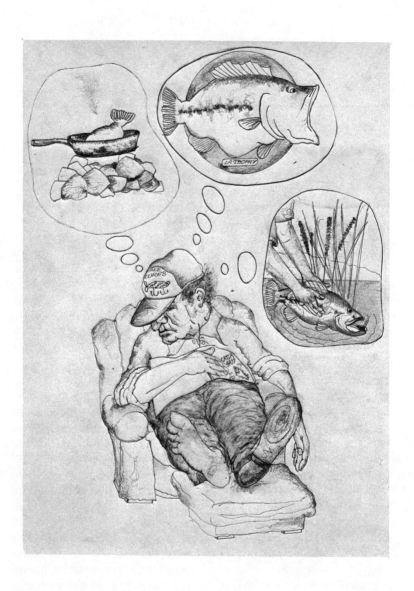

Your concept of a bass may vary, but we all share the dream of more and bigger fish.

1

Understanding Bass

- as a living thing -

AS A NEWCOMER to the exciting sport of bass fishing, you're eager to learn about the best places to fish, the right tackle, the proper presentations and lures to use to catch "Ol' Bucket-mouth." Perhaps your primary incentive to take up bass fishing is a desire to experience the outdoors. Bassin' will certainly ful-fill this objective, no matter where you live. Scenic Florida rivers, windblown Oklahoma reservoirs, tiny Ohio mining pits, secluded Iowa farm ponds, majestic Arizona canyon lakes — they all teem with bass! This widespread range of the bass, together with its great sporting qualities, make the largemouth the number one game fish in the United States. A multi-billion-dollar industry has grown up around the bass, and more people are bass fishing today than ever before.

But before you clear that spot on your mantel for a trophy bass, bear this in mind: *Bass fishing is tougher today than ever before. And it's getting even tougher!* There are several reasons for this. One is fishing pressure. We used to believe fishermen, even organized groups of anglers such as tournament fisher-men, could never put a serious dent in the bass fishery. Wrong! Scientific studies have proven that delayed mortality of bass released in fishing tournaments is a significant problem. Un-realistic state limits and "meat" fishing have taken their toll in many formerly productive waters. Trophy fishing has vastly reduced the numbers of big bass in areas such as Florida's fabled lakes and rivers. If fishing were easy, there would be no need for the computerized chart recorders, ultra-sensitive boron rods, and unending selection of lures that the industry churns out. After all, folks used to catch huge bass — hundreds of them — on cane poles, kinky braided lines, and unlikely looking lures!

Today's bass fisherman finds himself uttering this phrase with ever-increasing frequency: "Well, I didn't catch any, but I sure had a good time goin'!"

As a beginner basser it might be tempting after reading this to give up before you really get started. "If I'm not going to catch bass, why bother?" you might be asking yourself. On the contrary, as a beginner, you can catch bass from waters near your home, perhaps more bass than anglers who have fished these waters for years!

What's the secret? A magic lure? An ultra-sophisticated electronic gadget? *We believe the secret is understanding the bass as a living thing, and developing your fishing approach accordingly.*

Target vs. Living Thing

Today, a great many bass anglers, people who have fished for bass for years, never stop to think about the fish they seek to catch as a living creature. Instead, they think of the fish in other terms: tournament weight points, a potential stuffed trophy, something to show off to the guy next door. They aren't stopping to really think about the "target" they're aiming for! They catch a bass on a brushy point and don't stop to think about why that fish was there. They return to the launching ramp fishless on a cold, clear day and complain that they just couldn't find any fish. They catch a good bass on a stumpy bank in June, then return to the same spot later in the fall and wonder where the fish have gone.

The beginner, armed with the awareness that the bass is a living thing acting and reacting in an ecosystem with other living things, and backed by the knowledge of basic bass behavior can *catch bass* time after time, even when more experienced anglers fail!

Let's Look at the Bass

Even if you've never caught a bass, you know what they look like. You've seen your friends catch them, you've watched professional anglers on TV catch them. Yet, have you ever really looked at a bass? Understanding why a bass looks like it does will help you understand why it lives where it does, eats what it does, and acts like it does. And this knowledge can give you a head start toward successful bass fishing!

The bass' color and markings: Why is the largemouth bass colored and marked the way it is? Like most living creatures, the bass is camouflaged to fit into its surroundings. This helps explain why bass taken from weed-rich waters are greenish, and those from more open water appear brownish or even "pasty" looking, with few marks. The bass has the ability to alter its shades and hues to help conceal itself. It may appear mottled and black in shallow lilypads, or more golden and white as it moves into deeper water devoid of weeds. Smallmouth bass generally appear brown or bronze, because the smallmouth frequents rocky areas where it can find its favorite food, the crayfish.

The mouth of the largemouth bass is big enough to handle a vast variety of prey, including fish, aquatic birds, even some mammals. Here author Don Wirth admires an 11½-pounder he caught on a wild shiner from a Florida canal. The bass was tagged and released.   Photo by Doug Hannon

The bass' mouth: Perhaps its most identifiable feature, the mouth of a largemouth bass, is large in relation to the rest of its body . . . hence the common nickname, "bucketmouth"! What does this oversized mouth tell us about the fish? For one thing, it indicates that the largemouth bass is capable of feeding on a wide variety of prey as opposed to being a specialized feeder. Frogs, bluegills, carp, aquatic mammals, birds, minnows — a bass is capable of attacking and eating an amazing array of shapes, sizes, and species of prey. A 24-inch bass is fully capable of swallowing a 12-inch shiner . . . or bass! This capability of eating a wide variety of prey helps make the largemouth bass an extremely widespread and adaptable fish. It will feed actively on trout in deep California lakes, crayfish and shad in Tennessee reservoirs, and frogs in Michigan ponds. Its wide mouth will accept two particularly widespread forms of forage — bluegills and crayfish. It can swallow a short, round fish with sharp spines, like the bluegill; it can open its mouth wide enough to engulf an alarmed crayfish with its arms spread wide in its defense posture.

Can bass smell? Yes, but not nearly as well as can many other fish, especially catfish and trout. The use of so-called "worm dunks" or scented lure sprays by bass fishermen is of dubious value. We have proven in our field studies that a bass will attack a lure that presents strong visual cues, even though the lure has been dunked in a strongly repellent substance such as gasoline! This is not to suggest that bass cannot detect a foul odor, but rather indicates that they will ignore the input they receive from their olfactory organs if the input they receive from their visual organs is of sufficient strength.

How well can bass hear? To understand how well a bass can hear, we must first comprehend the amazing characteristics of sound in water. Sound travels almost five times as fast in water as it does in air: 4717 feet per second. Even more incredible is the fact that it travels with 100,000 times the efficiency. Two rocks clicked together can be heard over three miles away. For eons the great grey whales have been able to audibly communicate a low groaning sound frequency of about 20 hertz for distances of up to 6,000 miles! Even today, with boat traffic and all the noise pollution of modern shipping, these marine mammals can still communicate at ranges of over 200 miles. So much for the potential of sound transmission in water. As far as bass are concerned, suffice it to say that their hearing is excellent. Because of the efficiency of sound in water, there is nothing on land that even remotely compares to the bass' hearing, not even the fox, or the bat, or the mule deer. The bass has no external ear flaps or holes, simply because the sound passes through it just like water. You see, its body has a consistency and density very similar to water. On land, since our bodies are much denser than air, sound bounces off of us as well as off of any solid object. We therefore need ear flaps to gather sound and funnel it through an ear hole to the inner ear. The lack of an external ear, however, is not a handicap to the bass. Author Hannon's research makes him certain that a bass can hear the sound of an electric motor at several hundred yards, perhaps much farther in calm water. One of the most important facts to accept is that bass learn, and learn fast! In Hannon's tanks they will learn to feed out of his hand on cue in just a couple of days. Furthermore, they learn to recognize him as opposed to strangers. The speed of their learning is quite significant, since they must overcome many natural fears and cautions. Likewise, most reactions to sound are learned. Bass react to sound either positively or negatively; another bass struggling in distress makes them cautious while a school of bait feeding on the surface is a matter of great curiosity. With this in mind, it pays to emphasize caution when it comes to making noise while fishing. We cannot afford to assume that any noise is not offensive to bass, including the so-called "fish attracting" rattle built into some lures.

How well can bass see? The bass has an amazingly well-adapted pair of eyes that would be considered sophisticated in any part of the animal kingdom. Not only do they see very well, they also have forward-oriented eyes with good depth perception, like any predator. Their eyes are also very mobile so that they can see well in all directions with a minimum of body movement. All this implies that they depend heavily on their eyes for feeding and for catching prey. It is simply untrue to say that bass do not need their eyes and can serve all their feeding needs in total darkness. Bass can do some feeding without eyes, but not enough to successfully compete.

Can bass distinguish colors? Bass see colors very well and seem to express a preference to reds and an occasional aversion to yellows. Animals which center their activities after dark, like owls and cats, do not possess the ability to see color. Color cannot be seen at night because cones, the retinal cells which see color, are not sensitive enough to function at night. It takes so much light to fire the cone cell that having color vision means sacrificing some of your ability to see at night. As a result, the adaptation of color vision in the bass implies a heavy dependence on the eyes and on daylight feeding. Therefore, the color of your lure can be important, especially in shallow water where light is good and color resolution is high. As a rule, choose patterns which exaggerate natural color schemes, such as silver, gold, green, orange, blue, purple. Generally, reds and yellows are best used as a part of a lure's color scheme — for instance, as the skirt on a spinner, the belly on a plug, or the tail of a worm.

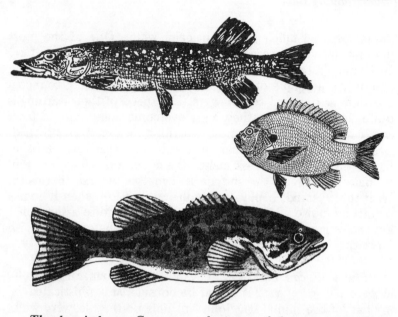

The bass' shape: Compare a largemouth bass to a northern pike and bluegill. The pike has a long, narrow body — hence the nickname, "snake." The bluegill has a short, rounded body typical of a panfish. Yet the largemouth bass seems to fall somewhere between these two extremes. It has a fairly wide body but not as wide and rounded as the bluegill's. It has a long body but not as long in relation to its width as the pike's. *The body shape of a fish tells us a great deal about its behavior and movements.* A pike or muskie feeds by lunging forward at tremendous speed to attack its prey. Its long, slim body shape facilitates fast forward movement. But these fish are incapable of great mobility. They depend on shooting out in short bursts to grab nearby food. They are often incapable of tracking down their food and chasing it over long distances, or of outmaneuvering escaping prey. The bluegill, on the other hand, is capable of tremendous mobility but little forward speed. If cornered, a bluegill will dodge and turn an amazing number of times in a small area in an attempt to escape; it knows that if it leaves a protected weedbed or brushpile, however, it will be an easy target in open water because it lacks forward speed. The largemouth bass, on the other hand, has a body shape which represents a *compromise* in many respects. It is capable of good forward speed, like the pike, but is able to swim long distances to track down its prey. The bass can swim at speeds of 18 mph, which is a very good speed in water. Besides fast forward speed, the bass has excellent maneuverability. When you consider that one of the favorite foods of the bass is the bluegill, its maneuverability becomes all the more apparent. The bass is capable of chasing down its prey, examining it, and eating it. It has perhaps the ultimate body shape for a combination of speed and maneuverability. This factor, again, helps account for its widespread range. It can chase down and eat all types of prey, including the wide-ranging bluegill.

Adaptability: The tremendous adaptability of the large-mouth bass helps account for its widespread range. Although a cold-blooded creature, the bass is capable of existing in a very wide range of water temperatures, more so than any other fish. Bass are caught in lakes with a surface temperature in the high 90s. Massachusetts' state record, a 15½-lb. bass, was taken through the ice! The peak activity range of the largemouth occurs in water temperatures from 80 to 82 degrees. As you are probably aware, the body temperature of a cold-blooded crea-ture is the same as the temperature of its surroundings. We'll see later in this book how water temperature is a prime factor in determining bass behavior and location.

The Life Cycle of the Bass

An awareness of how a bass lives in the changing seasons of the year will help you become a better fisherman. Bass, like other living things, are driven by the primal urges to mate and

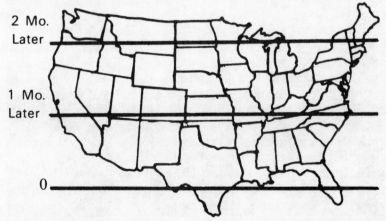

Based on the season in your location, you can determine the prevailing fishing season for any area of the country. This map is based on a horizontal line through central Florida. Since the sun advances northward 17 miles per day or 510 miles per month, so moves the seasons of the year.

spawn, to feed, and to protect themselves from danger. Their
world, a world of water, changes with the four seasons; so must
they change. They accomplish this by seeking the places that
offer them the most potential for fulfillment of their needs at a
given time of the year.

Spring: Somewhere around the full or new moon, when the
water temperature in a lake or river reaches about 60 degrees,
the male bass will move into the shallow waters in the northern-
most section of the body of water, seeking a hard, firm bottom
on which to make a nest. This northern, especially northwestern, area of the lake or river is the place that is first warmed
by the sun; water temperatures here will generally be 3 to 5
degrees higher than in other parts of that body of water. The
eggs need the sun to hatch. And in the spring, the sun is strongest in the northwestern section of the lake or river.

The spawning season generally lasts around six weeks, until
the water temperature rises above 72 degrees. It will occur as
early as late February in South Florida, to late May near the
Canadian border. Fishermen often complain that they had no
luck because "the bass are on the beds"; this is deceptive, for all
bass do not spawn at once, but rather the spawn occurs in
"waves" over a period of several weeks . . . *but always coinciding with the full or new moon.* The reason for this is that

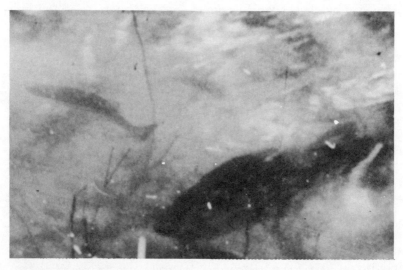

*A pair of spawning bass defend their nest. Note the large size of the female
in comparison to the male.*

bass, like other living things, use the moon as a "clock" to time their spawning activity. When great numbers of young are hatched at once, the chances of their being wiped out by predators are greatly decreased. More on the lunar influence in bass fishing in Chapter Seven.

The male fans out the nest on a firm bottom, using its tail. A mud bottom won't work; the silt would fall back to cover the eggs. After the nest has been made, the larger female bass begin entering the shallows. As with many fish, the female bass can get much larger than the male. Males seldom get bigger than 4 pounds; females may weigh 10 pounds or more. The females pick their mates and lay their eggs on the nests of their chosen males, where they are promptly fertilized by their mates. The female bass, contrary to popular belief, is very critical to the guarding of the nest and will often hang around for a few days to guard its eggs from many predators, notably bluegills, minnows, carp, turtles, and eels. The males take over the entire task just before hatching and the swarm of fry (which is much easier to protect than stationary eggs) is guarded by the male for a week or more.

Both male and female bass are very much "tuned in" to the nest at this crucial time; if disturbed, they can be observed swimming around in a circular fashion only to return to their nests, drawn back as if by a magnet. Bass are most easily observed during the spawning period. The nests are quite visible in shallow water as a light depression on the bottom. By walking down the bank or moving discreetly into the shallows in a boat, the females will often be seen guarding the nests; they are usually one-half the length of the nest. Bass are extremely aggressive at this time, and will readily attack anything — including your lure — should it come near the nest. The angler should keep in mind, however, that the fish are "glued" to these spots because of natural instincts at this time; the debate as to whether "bed fishing" is sportsmanlike will continue as long as fishermen fish for bass. The nests which have protective females around them have a much better chance of success; these are precisely the beds which a sportsman would not want to disturb.

After the eggs hatch — in four to seven days — the fry become instant targets for all sorts of predators. Bluegills, pike, minnows, other fish, birds, frogs, turtles — the list is seemingly endless. To escape predation, the fry seek the weedy areas of the shallows or places offering cover, which translates into *security* for the young bass: brushy areas, logjams or stump-fields, boathouses, etc. They feed on plankton and other tiny life forms, insects, and the like, until they grow to a size where they can begin to eat other fish, larger insects, etc.

Summer: As water temperatures rise to the high 80s and 90s, the bass becomes steadily less aggressive. Its body temperature also rises, and the fish has to be more careful of how much energy it expends. The bass becomes a more conservative creature, moving and feeding less. Its metabolism, sped up by the warmth of the water, causes it to expend a great deal of energy even while at rest. In 80-degree water, it takes a bass about four hours to digest its food. In 50-degree water, it takes four days! What do these facts tell us about where summer bass might be located? They have to eat more in hot water, yet they cannot move around as much. So *they pick locations in lakes and rivers where there is a vast abundance of easy-to-get food* . . . large schools of shad, for example. Prime spots for these feeding opportunities include brushy flats and points, weedy flats, and areas adjacent to two different environments — such as on the edge of the old river channel in a manmade reservoir. This gives the fish the opportunity to rest where food may pass from deep water into shallow, or from open water into cover. Typically, they will spend a great deal of time in holding places adjacent to structure in the areas mentioned, moving to attack a passing school of shad or other prey.

Fall: When the water temperature begins dropping, the bass can afford to become more active and aggressive. This fact makes the fall an exciting and productive time to catch bass. As weeds die off, the fish are forced to leave the summer flats and holding areas, and often congregate on long bars and points, then scatter to seek new holding areas. At this time, boat docks, logjams, gravel bars and points often hold scores of active fish. A larger lure often works better in the fall because the fish are feeding more actively and aren't so selective about what they eat.

Winter: Winter is typically a tough time to catch bass, but the angler armed with an understanding of where bass go and why they behave as they do in cold water, can take fish. Basically, the bass move to the deeper areas of the lake. However, this does not necessarily mean that they will be on the bottom in extremely deep water, say 60 feet deep or more. Instead, they tend to position themselves on steeply sloping banks, which allows them to move from deep to shallow water with a minimum of energy output. On a shallow flat, a bass may have to move a half mile to go from 6-to-9 feet of water; on a steep bank, a bass may only have to move a few feet to go from 35-to-8 feet. The deeper areas of the lake are not as subject to disorienting temperature shifts and other effects of cold fronts. In the winter, a bass reduces its food intake tremendously to match its greatly reduced metabolism. At this time, small lures, especially those fished right on the bottom, are the most productive (jigs, spoons, etc.).

How Cold Fronts Affect Bass: The Compression Factor.

The bass angler often speaks of a passing cold front as the reason why fishing was so tough. The latest scientific underwater observations of bass prove conclusively that there is indeed a reason for the tough fishing typical after a frontal passage. *Bass have been observed actually lying on their sides on the bottom at this time.* No wonder fishing is tough! There is a scientific explanation for this: the bass retreat to deeper water as the "bluebird skies" typical of a frontal passage move across the lake. The skies are blue because, after a frontal passage, there is very little humidity in the air. Humidity is nothing more than water vapor. And water is an excellent filter of ultraviolet light. When this "filter" is removed from the sun and the sky is clear, the fish, being extremely sensitive to ultraviolet light, simply can't stand it. They retreat deeper, to allow more water to separate them from the sun. Usually this can be accomplished by moving into water about 15 feet deep; however, the fish may go much deeper. Dropping down into deeper water in a hurry makes the air bladder of the bass compress, and the fish tend to "drop like rocks" to the bottom, where they may remain for two or three days until the air bladder readjusts. We call this phenomenon the "compression factor." If a fishing trip is planned in advance, the angler should take some care to consult the extended weather forecast for the area he's intending to fish, and reschedule if a cold front is imminent.

Bass and Objects

Bass are often referred to as *object-related* fish. This refers to their need to position themselves in, against, or near objects on the bottom or along shore; stumps, fallen trees, piles of brush, a large rock, etc. In a reservoir, many of these objects may be manmade: old house foundations, submerged roadbeds, old fence rows, etc. If you observe a bass in an aquarium, it will usually be found sitting against a stump or a rock, as opposed to a walleye, which roams nomadically around the tank in open water. Being a predator, the bass utilizes objects for security and as potential ambush points.

HANNON'S NORTHWEST FACTOR

"The northwest area of a lake in the northern hemisphere is the center of fish life and spawning activity."

Photo courtesy Mike Michaelis, Aeroimage, Palm Harbor, FL

A. The location is protected from seasonal northwest cold winds.

B. The southern angle of the sun provides more sun and less shade on the northern shore, thus increasing the water temperature by 3 degrees F. or more.

C. The added sun and warmth enriches plant life which provides food, oxygen, and shelter.

D. Increased plant life provides a dark-bottom condition which absorbs more of the sun's energy. (See photo)

Louisiana anglers work a stand of sparse brush, perfect bass habitat. In areas with a lot of similar cover, always look for "something different" — the place where one type of cover turns into another, or a lone bit of cover apart from a vast amount of similar cover.
— *B.A.S.S.* photo

Something Different

Often the bass angler gets excited when motoring to a likely fishing spot, only to leave disappointed at not catching a bass. A sprawling flat filled with brush, for example — you'd think there would be a bass behind every bush. Yet, when presented with a vast amount of seemingly identical cover, the bass will often select "something different" in its surroundings as a hiding or ambush point. For example, there may be a hundred feet of solid bushes with one lone bush twenty feet from the larger patch; the angler should always cast to that one lone bush before leaving the area. Similarly, on a mile-long, chunk rock bank, the bass will often gravitate to the place where the rock changes from fist-sized to basketball-sized, or to a cut or indentation in the bank. It's as though you entered a room with ten red chairs and one blue one, and for some reason unknown to you, felt more comfortable sitting in the blue one!

The Edge Effect

We mentioned earlier in this chapter the propensity for bass to relate to the edge, or the area adjacent to two different depths, structures, or habitats. In nature's world, many creatures occupy this niche. All creatures, predator and prey alike, seem to concentrate at the interface between two different environmental systems. For example, deer may inhabit the forests and rabbits the grassy plains. Because of the natural tendency to expand their range and avoid competition, they would each be concentrated on the edge of their territory. Predators such as wolves or bobcats often are attuned to the place where these two terrains come together. This gives them an expanded feeding opportunity. In the world of the bass, the edge might be a drop-off, weedline, the place where a stump field runs against a mud flat — any number of things. Fishermen should be alert to these places, and concentrate their angling activities in these potentially productive zones. Of course, don't overlook the biggest edge of them all — the shoreline!

"The edge" concept is dramatically visualized in this photo. Bill Dance, the "Babe Ruth of bass fishing," casts a crankbait into the edge of flooded timber in a Mississippi oxbow lake. Bass station themselves at the edge of two different environments to take advantage of the tremendous feeding opportunities present there.

— Photo by Don Wirth

What Is Structure Fishing?

Newcomers to the sport of bass fishing often hear the term "structure fishing" and are somewhat mystified as to its meaning. *Structure fishing is basically that fishing approach or point of view which recognizes that bass are creatures that relate to objects, something different, and the edge.* While a novice fisherman may just start out down a bank, casting with little awareness as to where bass might be hiding or stationed, a structure fisherman seeks to locate places containing situations ("structure") that would be potentially most conducive to holding bass. The term "structure" probably originated in the bass fishing boom of the sixties, when fishermen discovered they could move off the banks and find bass "out in the middle of the lake" on "structure" such as rock piles, fence rows, or submerged road beds, in manmade reservoirs. Today, the term has been broadened to include any place that bass might be found: a point in a natural lake is regarded as structure, as is a weedbed, a mound, a ledge, or a sandbar. The structure fisherman, to be successful, frequently depends on two tools — an electronic depth finder (flasher or chart recorder), and a topographic map. Often an experienced bass angler will review a topo map of the body of water he intends to fish, looking for manmade or natural structure. Then, once on the water, he will use his depth sounder to pinpoint the location.

Structure fishing has accounted for the tremendous growth of the bass fishing industry to a great degree. One would have little need for a $15,000 bass boat with a 150-horsepower outboard motor and sophisticated electronic gear if bass were readily found, clumped together like tomatoes on the vine in a convenient cove. Instead, fishermen seek out structure that holds bass in various parts of the lake. This hopping about to fish similar, often farflung structure, is known as "pattern fishing." A tournament angler seeks to put together the winning pattern in a short time. He does this by eliminating places where bass aren't and concentrating on those places where bass are. If this sounds overly obvious, consider all the places that could potentially hold bass in a given lake or river. There may be thousands! Yet the bass may be in only a few of these potential places at any given time. At certain times of the year, especially in the summer, bass tend to "bunch up" and relate very strongly to one type of structure or another. The angler who determines exactly what structure is holding bass, and who knows how to fish that structure effectively, will be rewarded with a sizeable catch in a short period of time.

Places where two or more favorable structures coincide or overlap are especially productive. The beginning angler may happen upon such a "honey hole" without realizing what he's found; an experienced tournament pro makes a career out of finding these places. For example, the place where an old road crosses a submerged creek channel — there's probably a demolished bridge down there, also. What a great place for bass! Finding these places will be easier as you grow to learn more about the bass and its favorite habitats.

How Bass Move

Bass are quite territorial, unlike crappie, walleye, salmon, or striped bass, which roam the lakes and rivers in vast nomadic schools comparable to the buffalo herds of yesteryear. Bass should also be viewed as individuals rather than members of a school. While they group together at certain times of the year to take advantage of certain feeding opportunities, they are mostly loners. There may be several bass on a given point, for example, but each has a definite place in the "pecking order" — they are not similar in their behavior, as are school fish. A bass may find a spot that suits its needs and remain there until caught by a fisherman or driven off by a larger bass or other predator. Of course, these favored spots change as do the seasons. An individual bass may have a favored stump in shallow water during the spring, a favored brushy flat in the summer, and so forth.

When bass move about a body of water, they tend to follow underwater "road maps" such as the old river channel, a submerged roadbed, a weedline, or — especially — the shoreline, rather than scattering without rhyme or reason. However, it would be incorrect to picture the bass as a creature covering vast areas of water in its yearly movements. *Bass tend to live in areas that have the most favorable elements close together.* The angler who can find these areas may tap into the greatest potential any given body of water has to offer. Scientific tracking studies in which microtransmitters are imbedded in bass and their movements tracked electronically, indicate that largemouth bass may move only a few hundred yards over the period of a year or more, and generally follow the shoreline! It stands to reason, then, that they would want to live in a place that offers excellent spawning habitat, deeper water for summer and winter, and an expanse of flats, points, weeds, brush, etc. for hiding and ambushing prey. Smallmouth bass are even more territorial than are largemouths; a smallmouth in prime waters such as Tennessee's Dale Hollow Lake may reach nine or ten pounds and live fifteen years or more . . . without ever leaving an area 400 yards from where it was born!

Where Do World Records Live?

Every angler has fantasies of catching a world record fish, and bass fishermen are no exception. The world record largemouth was caught by George W. Perry from Montgomery Lake, an oxbow off Georgia's Ocmulgee River, on June 2, 1932. Perry's monster bass weighed 22 lbs. 4 oz. On March 4, 1980, Raymond D. Easley caught a 21 lb. 3 oz. largemouth from Lake Casitas in California; Easley's fish is the current International Game Fish Association (IFGA) certified world record bass for its line class (8 lb. line) and is the largest officially certified largemouth bass caught in recent history. The world record smallmouth bass, 11 lbs. 15 oz., was caught on July 9, 1955, by David L. Hayes in Dale Hollow Reservoir, Kentucky, Tennessee. Every year, the outdoor press hears reports about new world record bass caught from obscure ponds or famous lakes; in many cases, the anglers claim to have eaten their prizes, not realizing what they had caught. Baloney! With the amount of money involved in prizes and endorsements, no world record bass claim should be believed unless it has been certified by the IFGA.

Still, world record bass *do* exist and it is possible for records to be broken, but it's becoming more unlikely with each passing day. Why? Because prime bass habitat, habitat capable of supporting the growth of a bass to world record size, is rapidly disappearing due to pollution, industrialization, and the ever-advancing encroachment of the primary enemy of the bass: man. We are often asked where, in our opinion, the next world record largemouth will come from. The potential of stocking Florida bass in other states' waters cannot be denied, but we believe it may well come from a river, not a lake. A river offers several factors which are potentially conducive to the growth of a world record bass, especially the short, pure rivers such as the Withlacoochee or the Oklawaha in Florida: a river has moving water which tends to carry the food to the bass. A bass in a river has to expend less energy tracking down its food. It will station itself out of the current, behind a large rock, piling, and the like, and wait for food to drift by, rushing out and

ambushing it. Life in a river demands less energy output compared to the potential food intake. In general, a river, if not
polluted, has more oxygen than a lake, and this oxygen is
usually mixed from top to bottom, as opposed to a lake where
the oxygen tends to stratify in the top layers unless the water
is exceptionally clear. In fact, a typical river may have twice
as much oxygen as a lake! And oxygen is essential for life.
Therefore, a river has more life than a lake . . . more plankton,
more minnows, more crayfish, and the potential for more bass
in the same relative amount of water. For a fish to grow to
world record size, the water must not get too warm or too
cold. Florida's scenic rivers offer a great potential for world
record fish when viewed from this regard; moving water has
more evaporation taking place than calm water, and evaporation serves to keep the water cool. Some of Florida's spring-fed
rivers have a constant surface temperature of only 73 degrees.
Rivers have plenty of shade from overhanging trees; this helps
keep them cooler, too. And finally, certain areas of rivers
simply may be too remote for all but the most determined
anglers to attempt fishing in them. We believe that the next
world record bass will come from a body of water — probably
a river — located somewhere between Gainesville and Tampa,
Florida. This is the fabled "big bass belt" of the United States
and it's the area that offers the most potential for having a
record-class bass. A few miles south of this range, at sprawling
Lake Okeechobee, for example, the water simply gets too hot
to support a lot of truly huge bass. A 10 lb. fish is rare at Lake
Okeechobee; we have personally taken fish exceeding 16 lbs.
from rivers between Gainesville and Tampa, and have been eye-
witness to bass larger than this in this same locale. We feel that
the potential for world record fish to occur in extreme southern locales such as Cuba or Honduras is unlikely; the water
there simply gets too hot to allow the fish to live long enough
to grow to world record size.

Smallmouth bass need plenty of deep cool water, gravel
and rocks; and crayfish, plus extremely pure water with plenty
of oxygen. Dale Hollow provides all of these; we'd wager the
next world record smallmouth would come from there or from
one of the nearby Middle Tennessee deepwater reservoirs that
offer much the same type of habitat (Center Hill, Woods, or
Percy Priest reservoirs).

Daydreaming about world record bass is part of the mystery
and excitement of fishing for them; however, daydreams some-

times get in the way of facts. For example, many anglers point to the deep California reservoirs around San Diego as places where the next world record fish may come from; Ray Easley's 21 lb. 3 oz. bass would certainly lend credence to this claim. Also, there have been reports of fish of world record proportions found floating dead in these lakes. However, California and its Florida transplants have at least one thing going against them in a bid to produce a 22 lb. 6 oz. largemouth (the minimum weight acceptable by the IFGA to replace Perry's bass as the new all-tackle world record largemouth): *The fish there don't grow long enough.* Their staple diet appears to be trout, which, for some reason, aren't putting sufficient skeletal growth on the bass. Perry's world record was 5 inches longer than Easley's. California lunkers are typified by massive potbellies; huge Florida bass are far longer. That's not to say that no potential world record bass now swims in California. It's to say that there are far more of them swimming in Florida . . . and therefore, a far greater potential for one to be caught, and the record to be broken.

Summing Up:
Viewing the Bass as a Living Thing

Understanding the bass as a living thing will give you far greater potential as a successful bass angler than if you viewed the fish as a lone "target" or "object." Knowing how and why bass interact with other creatures in their aquatic environment, and react to such factors as sunshine, water temperature, frontal passages, and the changing seasons, can help you put the pieces of the bass fishing puzzle together. Even fishermen who have fished for bass with some success for years may not be aware of the information you have just read. Knowing why you caught a bass at a certain time and place will help you gain success and enjoy bass fishing more.

When starting to acquire fishing gear, it's best to choose a store with a large tackle selection. A shop with a limited inventory will sell you what's in stock, not necessarily what you need.

CHAPTER

2

Basic Bass Tackle

THE NEWCOMER to the sport of bass fishing, upon entering a sporting goods store, is quickly confused and overwhelmed by the vast array of bass fishing rods, reels, lines and lures. This is because the bass is such a widespread and generalized fish; if it were highly specialized, like a muskie, only certain, more limited kinds of equipment would be required. Our intent in Chapter Two is to describe the basic types of rods, reels, and line you are likely to encounter, not to suggest that you go out and buy every possible combination or type on the market. You can catch bass using very little equipment when you know how; in fact, one good rod and reel may be all you'll need.

Where To Shop: The specialized sporting goods store with a complete selection of fishing equipment, staffed by knowledgeable and helpful personnel, is being replaced by the high-volume, lower-cost discount store. For the beginner, this makes shopping for the right bass tackle difficult, because a discount store stockboy probably won't be able to help you decide between a Fenwick or a Daiwa rod. Still, specialized fishing shops are around. It pays to seek them out and ask their advice. Once you know what you need, discount stores and mail-order outlets can save you money.

Ask Other Fishermen: If you have a friend who has the reputation of being a good bass angler, seek his or her advice on which tackle to buy. People who fish a lot find that second-rate gear simply won't hold up to the rigors of bassin', especially tournament fishing. Attend the weigh-in at a local bass tournament and observe the kind of tackle the participants are using. Serious pro tournament anglers cannot afford to spend valuable time hassling with malfunctioning equipment; their livelihoods depend on the right tackle. Articles in such magazines as *Bassmaster* often tell what the pros use and how they use it; such input can be valuable information to the newcomer seeking to invest in superior equipment.

Buy Wisely: While we don't suggest you immediately rush out and buy the most expensive and elaborate bass tackle available, neither do we suggest you buy the cheapest. You would be better off with one good quality rod and reel than a half-dozen cheapies. Good tackle is easier to cast, more sensitive to the often light strike of a bass, more durable to the hard knocks of bassin', and more fun to use. Good tackle gives you pride of ownership that makes bass fishing more pleasurable. Cheap tackle? It'll just ruin your day. Compared to many other sports such as golf or skiing, bass fishing equipment is relatively inexpensive. We suggest you buy the best tackle you can afford; you'll probably pass it along to your grandchildren one day.

Bass Fishing Reels

What is the Purpose of a Reel? A fishing reel has three functions: it must cast, hold, and gather line. Bass fishing reels must have certain features that allow them to fulfill specific needs. A large line capacity is not one of these; bass, unlike salmon or many salt-water species, don't make tremendously long runs when hooked. However, a bass reel must be able to cast lures of varying weights. Common bass lures weigh from 1/4 ounce to an ounce or more. The reel also must be capable of reeling in a fish and allow for line slippage when the fish pulls harder than the line tests. This function is called the drag, and a reliable smooth drag is an absolute must in bassin'. A bass reel should have a simple, corrosion-free mechanism. A good bass reel will last a lifetime.

Spincast Reels: Typically, this is the kind of equipment most fishermen first experience. It is the equipment used by more fishermen than any other; it is also the least favored among more experienced and knowledgeable anglers. There are not many top quality spincast reels available, simply because more of the latest technology in the tackle industry is directed where the most profit exists: in baitcasting reels.

Spincast reels work by the push of a button. The angler pushes the button on the reel, makes his cast, and releases the button. This is a very simple procedure, which accounts for the popularity of spincast reels among novice anglers. Still, spincast fishing has real disadvantages. It isn't as accurate as either spinning or baitcasting, and accuracy in bass fishing is of primary importance because bass often won't move far from their cover. You can use only lighter lines effectively on spincast gear, and bass fishermen often need 17 lb. test or higher when fish are in heavy cover. Spincast reels are relatively back-lash-free, however. But, as we'll see, advances in baitcasting gear have all but eliminated this bane of the bass fisherman.

One real advantage of starting out on spincast gear is that you may someday wish to graduate to a baitcasting reel; if you have a good quality rod, you can use it with either type of reel.

Spincast reels are popular with beginning bass fishermen; as the angler's fishing skill grows and he moves up to baitcasting, the same rod may be used with both types of reels.

Garcia photo

Spinning Reels: Spinning reels utilize a wire bale to pick up the line and gather it back on the stationary spool. Like the spinning wheels of yore, the bale weaves your line into place on the spool. Spinning reels are typically used in bass fishing for light-line fishing and will handle 8, 6, 4, even 2 lb. tests with ease, permitting the angler to use tiny lures that he would be unable to cast with a spincast or baitcasting reel. Spinning gear is most often used by bass fishermen in extremely clear water when light line is required to fool a wary bass. It's an excellent choice for winter fishing, when the bass' metabolism has slowed to a point where it will accept only small, bottom-bumping lures like 1/8 oz. jigs. At this time, the use of lighter line will make it easier to fish your lures deeper.

The Cardinal, an extremely popular spinning reel, is perfectly suited to lines from 4 to 10 lbs.

Garcia photo

While spinning reels do not backlash, they are prone to line twist, especially when a big fish pulls out a lot of line and the drag slips. You'll find you must be extremely "line conscious" when using light spinning gear, changing your line more frequently. Light line is more subject to abrasion and break-off than is the 17 lb. test "well rope" you use on your baitcasting rig. If you fish both fresh and salt water, you might consider a beefy, surf-type rod of 7 ft. or longer with a salt-water spinning reel; pro angler Tom Mann has successfully competed on the tournament trail with such an outfit for years.

Skirted Spools are advantageous when considering a spinning reel; most of the latest models have them. The spool overlaps the retrieve mechanism in such a way that it is impossible for a line to get under the spool, a common occurrence in traditional spool designs.

Baitcasting Reels: Perhaps the classic bassin' reels are the level-wind baitcasting reels; your grandfather probably relied on a reel like this. It's a choice that's hard to top in the world of bass fishing. With a level-wind baitcasting reel, you can (1) fish a wide variety of line weights on the same reel to meet changing conditions, (2) cast more accurately than with any other type of reel, and (3) enjoy a lifetime of service — properly cleaned and lubricated, the simple mechanism of a baitcasting reel should last a lifetime.

Magnetic spool baitcasting reels provide even the novice basser with backlash-free operation.

Garcia photo

With a baitcasting reel the line comes off and goes on the same way; as a result, you get very little line twist. The bane of baitcasting has traditionally been backlash; first-timers are horrified by a tangled "professional overrun" and may never again pick up a baitcasting reel. But with today's baitcasting equipment, even an angler who has never made a cast before can easily learn to use a baitcasting rig.

The totally backlash-free reel has yet to be invented, but the latest magnetic baitcasting reels are the closest thing to it. They are the choice of the professional angler, yet they bring all the benefits of baitcasting to the novice because they are so simple and foolproof to use. Backlash is caused when the spool keeps turning after the lure stops, and because the lure slows down after it is cast due to air resistance. That is why back-lashes commonly occur on windy days — naturally, the spool doesn't slow down because of wind resistance; it keeps turning at its normal rate, causing line to pay out faster than the lure flies. Magnetic baitcasting reels such as the Daiwa Mag Force series have tiny magnets built into the reel that allow precise control of the forward movement of the spool, far more precise than even an expert caster could ever exercise with his thumb. They allow you to dial the exact amount of backlash control needed for varying lure weights and wind conditions. We highly recommend them to both novice and professional alike. They're high-tech fishing machines that are far more compact, lighter in weight, and more precise than their predecessors. They are also more expensive. However, for those beginning bassers intent on getting off on the right track, no finer reels are available.

Loading Line: Monofilament line has a "memory"; that is, it tends to roll off its stored spool with a curvature, and this must be taken into account when loading your reels. When loading line on a baitcasting reel, simply put a pencil through the hole in the spool, stick the pencil in a vise or have a friend hold it, and reel the line off the spool, securing the end of the line to the spool in the direction of its memory. For spinning or spincasting reels, set the spool face up on the floor, secure the line to the spool in the direction of its memory, and reel 20 turns. Now look at the line coming off the storage spool. If it appears twisted, turn the spool over and continue reeling.

Bass Fishing Rods

What is the Purpose of the Rod? The fishing rod facilitates the throwing (casting) of lures by acting as a springy extension of your arm. It also acts as a shock absorber between the fish and your line. Should a fish hit your lure, the rod must give slightly to keep the line from breaking.

Qualities of a Good Bass Rod: In general, the beginning basser often buys a rod which is too whippy or soft in action for bass fishing. Novices often select a rod primarily for its casting ability, not its sensitivity and fish-catching abilities. *A fairly stout rod is needed to feel a strike, to properly set a hook, and to control a powerful bass, especially one hooked in heavy cover.* Most bass rods are between 5½ and 6 ft. long. This is short by comparison with many types of rods, such as salt-water tackle or salmon gear. A shorter, stiffer rod is a more accurate caster. Because bass are object-related fish, as we have seen, accurate casting often makes the difference between fishless trips and success. Shorter rods are far easier to handle in a boat and when bank fishing also. A good bass rod generally has what is known as a fast tip. This means that when the rod is swept back, as when setting a hook, the tip of the rod has very little bow or "give" to it; the tip sweeps back just about as fast as the rest of the rod. This is highly desirable in bass fishing. When using soft, plastic baits such as plastic worms, which almost always are used with single hooks, the angler must drive home the hook upon detecting a strike; a rod with a fast tip both telegraphs the strike and allows a more powerful hook-set than a softer-action rod. You will see rods with actions labeled "worm action"; these are powerful rods with extremely fast tips, generally 5½ ft. long. If you buy but one bass rod, we recommend as a good compromise a medium to medium-heavy action. This will allow you to fish with a wide variety of lures and line tests.

Composition of Bass Rods: The beginner will be further confronted with the decision to purchase a rod made of fiberglass, graphite, or boron. Let's examine the merits and disadvantages of each. Remember that part of the extra expense of rods made from the more exotic materials comes from the fact that they all tend to use the best guides and handles and are commonly manufactured as premium equipment.

Fiberglass Rods — Advantages: Fiberglass rods are (1) relatively inexpensive — you can buy a good fiberglass bass rod for $15 to $25, (2) fairly light and reasonably strong, (3) flexible and not brittle in cold weather, (4) durable and long-lasting. — *Disadvantages:* (1) They are heavier than other kinds of rods available today, and (2) they aren't as sensitive as other rods.

Graphite Rods — Advantages: (1) Moderately priced — many are now available for under $30, and (2) lighter and more sensitive than fiberglass. *—Disadvantages:* (1) Brittle and prone to breaking, especially in cold weather, (2) not as sensitive as boron, and (3) relatively stiff.

Boron Rods —Advantages: (1) Very strong and durable, not brittle, (2) the most sensitive rods available, and (3) the lightest rods available. *—Disadvantages:* (1) Expensive compared to other types of rods, and (2) relatively stiff.

Rod Composition — Choices Analyzed: In general, we feel the bass fisherman should limit his rod choices to either fiberglass or boron, with boron being the preferred composition. We feel graphite is a poor choice for rods. Boron is more expensive but so far superior that graphite is being eased out of the lineups of many tackle manufacturers. Of course, as boron becomes more prevalent, prices should fall. As we go to press, a good quality boron rod retails for $75 or more. Fiberglass rods are to be found in the arsenals of even tournament professionals; they often prefer them for spinnerbaits and buzz baits, where some "give" is desired when a bass inhales the bait. If one rod is to be purchased, shop carefully and strongly consider the boron rods available today; they simply can't be beat for durability, lightness, and sensitivity. A medium to medium-heavy boron rod, 5½ to 6½ ft., coupled with a magnetic bait-casting reel, should cost the beginner around $150 or less and will provide a lifetime of fishing pleasure.

Spinning Rods for Bass: Again, select a spinning rod with a strong butt and fast tip for bass fishing, not a light or ultra-light (UL) action. Two spinning rods we've tried with great success are Charlie Brewer's Slider rod, available in four lengths, and the Billy Westmorland spinning rod, available from Bass Pro Shops (see Appendix for addresses). They are ideally suited for use with spinning reels such as the Cardinal 4, Shimano Quickfire X2000 or MLX 200, etc., with 6 to 8 lb. test. You'll find either rod series capable of handling very big fish; author Wirth once landed a 17 lb. drum in heavy current on a Slider fiberglass rod with the Shimano MLX 200 and 6 lb. line. Spinning tackle is best suited for relatively open-water bassin' or when the water is very clear and light lines and small lures are necessitated; it is the standard method employed by smallmouth bass fishermen in deep, clear lakes.

Lines

The function of the line is to provide a connecting link between you and the lure . . . and ultimately, between you and the bass. We bring up this seemingly obvious point to make you aware that your line may be the weakest link separating you from a fish. Unfortunately, the only time many anglers think about their line is *after* they've hooked a trophy fish! It's a sinking feeling to have hooked the fish of a lifetime only to have your line break because you failed to retie after scraping it against logs, rocks, and other obstructions during the day's fishing. *Be a line checker!* It takes just a second to run your fingers along your line, particularly the 18 inches above your lure. Clip it off and retie occasionally if you detect nicks and abrasions.

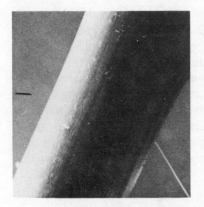 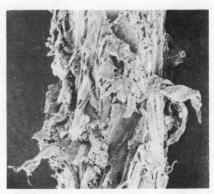

Check your line often to make sure it hasn't been weakened by line abrasion. The line on the left side is new, 10-lb. test nylon monofilament, magnified 200 times using an electron microscope. The line on the right is the same type line, only it has been heavily fished.

Photo courtesy of Berkley & Co.

Which Brand to Buy? Lines have been the object of tremendous discussion among bassers, and claims from the various manufacturers as to the superiority of their products have clouded the issue. Suffice it to say that *all premium lines available today are excellent choices for bass fishing.* Line technology has advanced, and the competition is so fierce, you can rest assured of a superior quality bassin' line if you choose from Stren, Trilene, Maxima, or other premium brands. Your line is the last place to skimp to save money. Cheap monofilament lines tend to be very stiff and hard to cast, and retain their spool memory a long time, causing short casts and backlashes.

Here are the qualities of a premium monofilament line, all available in the top brand names mentioned: (a) Low Visibility — select a line that the fish can't see. Author Hannon has done extensive underwater photography and reports that in some water conditions, fluorescent lines glow like a neon tube under water! Choose a pale green, pale brown, or a clear line, but *stay away from the fluorescents.* Surprisingly, lines with a little color are less visible than clear lines. Avoid gold, orange, or yellow lines. (b) Stretch — premium lines have a slight degree of stretch, which is desirable. If line did not stretch, it would break when setting a hook; lines that stretch too much lose their hooking power. (c) Abrasion Resistance — bass, being the predatory creatures that they are, will often be found in heavy cover, necessitating a line that will hold up to abrasion.

What Test Line Should I Use? The answer to this question depends on what kind of rod and reel you're using, what kinds and weights of lures you're using, and what kind of water you'll be fishing. *Generally speaking, on a baitcasting outfit, start with 12 to 14 lb. test; 8 lb. on a spinning outfit; and 10 on a spincast.* The most popular baitcasting line size among tournament pros is 14; this, of course, will vary as to conditions. The authors have fished alongside the pros many times in such national tournaments as the Bass Masters Classic; a "typical" pro tournament baitcasting outfit would be a boron rod, magnetic baitcasting reel, and 14 lb. test.

Favorite Bass Fishing Knots:

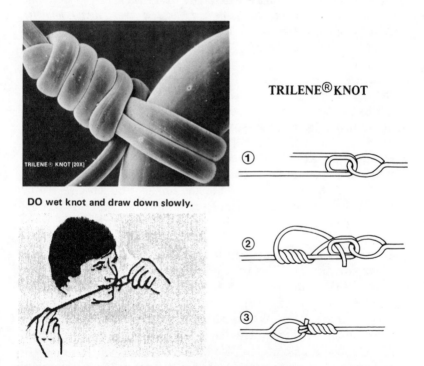

TRILENE® KNOT [20X]

DO wet knot and draw down slowly.

TRILENE® KNOT

① ② ③

The Trilene® knot's unique design and ease of tying yields consistently strong, dependable knots of 85-90% of the original line strength. The double wrap of mono through the eyelet provides a protective cushion and an added safety factor. Use this knot when you want a high strength, reliable connection that resists slippage and premature failures. It is a general purpose connection knot to be used in joining monofilament to swivels, snaps, hooks, and artificial lures.

Courtesy of Berkley & Co.

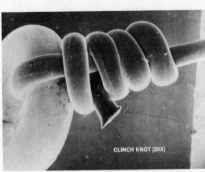

IMPROVED CLINCH KNOT

Best knot for multiple hook lures.

PALOMAR KNOT

Best knot for jigs and single-hook lures.

Sharpen Your Hooks!

With bass fishing getting tougher every day, you don't want to blow any chance you might have for a big bass. One easy way to increase your odds of landing that lunker is to sharpen your hook! The jawbone of a big bass is extremely tough, and it often takes both a powerful hook-set and an extremely sharp hook to penetrate and hold. Follow the illustrations below for sharpening your hook. Remember, it's not sharp enough unless it hangs up on your fingernail when you drag it across!

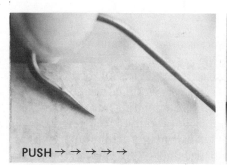
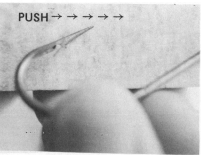

Proper sharpening requires that the hook be pushed point first across a good stone. Use the angle shown in the photos and be sure to sharpen both sides.

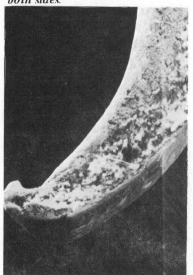

Electron microscope photos (60x) of dull versus sharp hook points.
Photo courtesy of Berkley & Co.

Bass Lures

IF YOU THINK it's confusing to shop for rods and reels, wait until you enter that sporting goods store and eyeball the thousands of different types, sizes, and colors of bass lures! Most beginning bass fishermen either get overly confused about selecting the correct baits, or end up spending more than is necessary. The aim of this chapter is to put together a basic bassin' tacklebox, an assortment of lures that, while not representing a major investment, will certainly catch bass under all the situations you're likely to encounter.

Plastic Worms — The Ultimate Bass Lures

Perhaps the single most effective artificial bait for bass, all things considered, is the plastic worm. Since its introduction in the fifties, the plastic worm has accounted for more big bass than all other artificial lures combined. *It's our top recommendation for huge bass (over 15 lbs.).* In spite of its popularity, the plastic worm is often misused and misunderstood. Many beginners express frustration because they cannot get the hang of using it.

There are several effective ways to fish a plastic worm. Unfortunately, most fishermen limit themselves to only one of them — the Texas rig. Let's examine the various worm fishing alternatives you should learn to catch bass under varying situations.

The Texas Rig: This worm fishing technique received its name from its popularity during the tremendous bass boom of the sixties at Texas' Toledo Bend and Sam Rayburn reservoirs. It incorporates a slip sinker ahead of the worm and utilizes a hook of varying size and design which is buried in the body of the worm to make it weedless. To fish the Texas rig, follow these steps: (1) Using a medium-heavy to heavy rod, 14 lb. line minimum, and a baitcasting reel, cast out the worm and allow it to settle to the bottom. (2) When the line goes slack, lift the rod to approximately a "one o'clock" position. (3) *Without dropping the rod,* allow the worm to fall back to the bottom. Many strikes occur at this time; if you dropped the rod, the line would go slack and you could not feel the strike. (4) Repeat the procedure until the worm has been retrieved. Again, the biggest mistake most anglers make when fishing the Texas rig is dropping the rod before the worm has settled back to the bottom. Practice these easy maneuvers next time you go fishing and enjoy more strikes!

Setting the Hook on a Texas Rig: The angler fishing in productive bass water should soon be rewarded with a tell-tale TAP TAP! signaling that a bass has inhaled the lure. Notice we use the term "inhaled"; a bass will take a worm by swimming up to it and flaring its gills open wide. This causes a rapid intake of water, sand, silt, and your lure as the whole works enters the bass' mouth as though sucked into a vacuum cleaner! Newcomers to the sport often ask, "How long should you let a bass run before setting the hook?" The answer is, Not very long! Hit the bass immediately upon detecting the strike.

A common mistake of many fishermen is to feel the strike, then tighten down on the bass, "feeling" if it's still there before setting the hook. *More big bass have been lost this way than perhaps by any other angling mistake involving lures!* Instead, drop your rod tip abruptly and bring it back overhead sharply. This is known as the slack-line hookset. It serves to drive home the hook sharply. It's common for the novice angler detecting a strike on a worm to wait until the bass pulls the line tight before attempting to set the hook. Often the fisherman is rewarded with the memory of a big bass head emerging from the water, turning and throwing the bait. Use a slack-line hookset and avoid such memories.

Choosing the Right Sinker: Perhaps the most popular sinker for the Texas rig is a ¼ oz. slipsinker. In theory, when the bass picks up the worm, it can carry it away while the line pays out through the holes in the sinker; the bass, therefore, cannot feel its weight (although this probably is not a factor with weights under ¾ oz.). In deeper water, a heavier sinker is more efficient, up to ¾ oz. In extremely clear and shallow water, we have used slipsinkers as light as 1/64 oz.

Pegging the Sinker: Often the slipsinker will hang around a branch or other obstruction in heavy cover. This can be eliminated by pegging the sinker. Simply insert a small piece of toothpick into the hole of the sinker nearest the worm; the sinker now will not slide. Of course, the drawback is that with a very heavy sinker, the bass can feel its weight. Pegging is often used when flipping a worm in dense cover (more on flipping later).

Texas Rig Hooks: Many excellent worm hooks are available for Texas rig worm fishing. We recommend Tru-Turn hooks and the Mustad-type hooks with a 40 degree angle of penetration. But, no matter what hook you select, sharpen it religiously, using the instructions in the previous chapter. We're often asked how big a hook to use. We prefer a 1/10 or 2/0 hook, which is smaller than that used by many fishermen. A smaller hook, when sharpened to a razor edge, is easier to set in a big bass.

The Swimmin' Worm: The swimmin' worm is best used in shallow water. Instead of fishing it on the bottom like a Texas rig, it is brought back to the boat using a slow, steady retrieve. The trick to fishing the swimmin' worm is proper rigging so that the worm rolls as it comes through the water. Use an Eagle Claw #186 hook, size #1, and a small (6-inch) plastic worm with no frills (the Creme Scoundrel is our favorite). The worm is threaded onto the hook through the head and out the egg-sack so that the hood protrudes. Next, roll the body of the worm so that the body is bent and the hood protrudes inside that bend, making it weedless (see illustration). Next, take 14 inches of 30-lb. monofilament and tie it to the hook as a leader (this extremely heavy line facilitates your being able to fish the rig around heavy cover without having to constantly retie). Attach this leader to your regular fishing line (12 to 17 lb. test) and cast the swimmin' worm around weedlines, grass-beds, or other cover in shallow water. Retrieve with a slow, steady action, carefully watching the worm as it swims and rolls back to the boat — bass may often be sighted as they attack the bait! *The swimmin' worm is the best artificial bait we have ever used in shallow, weedy situations such as in Florida's natural lakes.* We have documented three bass over 17 lbs. on this lure, which is highly unusual for an artificial.

The Do Nothing Rig: Professional tournament angler Jack Chancellor of Phenix City, Alabama, has recently revived the old "Carolina" worm rig and added a few twists of his own, calling it the Do Nothing worm. It is perhaps the most blatantly

misnamed lure ever made; it does something, alright — it catches
bass! Let's let Chancellor tell you how to fish it in his own
words: "The Do Nothing rig is the lure that has put me in the
money in many national bass tournaments, including the Bass
Masters Classic. It is an unusual looking rig, and may be rather
unwieldy for the beginning angler to cast. However, with a little
practice, you'll find it an extremely exciting and productive
lure. It's easy to fish and catches a lot of fish. In fact, I caught
100 bass a day on this lure during a recent Classic.

"The Do Nothing worm is a very small (4 inches) translucent
worm with a braided nylon cord running through its body,
forming a loop which protrudes at the head. Attached to the
cord are two tiny hooks. To the loop, tie approximately 5 ft.
of 12 lb. line as a leader. Next, tie on the large swivel. To your
regular 14 to 20 lb. line, attach an extremely heavy (1 oz.)
slipsinker and a tiny red plastic bead. Tie your regular line to
the other end of the large swivel. It's rather ungainly to cast at
first but easy once you get the hang of it. Using a stiff-arm cast,
hurl the rig out over a point, sandbar, ledge, or other likely
location. The sinker will sink rapidly with a tell-tale thump.
Retrieve the lure by simply reeling in at a slow to medium
rate, not trying to impart any other action to the lure . . . just
reel! The sinker will scoot along the bottom, kicking up little
clouds of silt. Occasionally, it will hang up on a rock or other
obstruction; when this happens, simply keep reeling, tightening
down. Eventually the sinker will work free and scoot forward.
As the sinker hops, bounces, and scoots along, the little worm,
which tends to suspend in the water, will dart and settle in a
manner extremely enticing to the fish. A strike will often occur
just after the sinker works free and the worm darts forward;
strikes often feel like the fish is "gobbling" the lure. When a
strike occurs, do not rear back and set the hook as in Texas rig
fishing; you'll rip the tiny hooks right out of the bass. Instead,
simply keep on reeling; the bass will hook itself because the
small hooks are very sharp and penetrate easily. Always adjust
your reel's drag so that it will slip when using this rig. It may be
helpful to use a special-purpose rod with a long handle for Do
Nothing fishing. Once mastered, you should catch a lot of bass
when you Do Nothing!"

Other Worm Methods: The plastic worm is an extremely
adaptable lure. The angler can modify it or rig it in endless ways
to suit special circumstances. Here are a couple of our favorites
that you ought to experiment with:

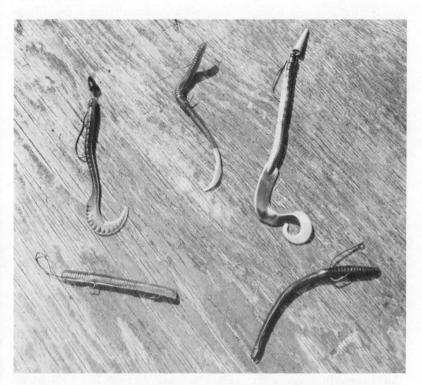

Plastic worms (clockwise from top left): Texas rig with sliding sinker; Hannon "swimming worm" rig; Texas rig with "Burke Slinker" weight; "Swinging" worm rig; and Chancellor "Do Nothing" worm.

The Swingin' Worm: Try this close to cover and in extremely clear water, especially in tight places such as beneath an overhanging tree. Take a 6-inch Creme Scoundrel or other plain plastic worm and, using a 3/0 to 5/0 hook, drive the hook sideways through the worm about 1½ inches down from the head. Use no weight. Cast the lure under a tree and jiggle the rod tip. It will imitate a writhing caterpillar.

Sliders: The Slider is a small plastic worm manufactured by Charlie Brewer in Lawrenceburg, Tennessee. The worm is actually only half of the bait; it is fished on a Slider head, an oval, flat leadhead with the eye riding straight up. Sliders may be rigged in innumerable ways; they are one of the most versatile and effective bass lures we've run across. Brewer also manufactures a rod specially designed for his Slider fishing system. The fiberglass version (our favorite) is one of the finest spinning rods made for bass. Slider heads are available in various weights; we recommend using a 1/4 or 1/8 oz. head and cutting it down to size with pliers if you want it to fall slower, which is desirable in cold water. The head may be trimmed to any shape desired, and may be flattened to vary the rate of fall. Unlike a typical Texas rig worm which is fished on the bottom, the Slider is cast and allowed to fall to the desired depth, then reeled in slowly without imparting any action whatsoever to the lure. The tiny worm will come through the water like a stick; amazingly enough, bass eat 'em up! Actually, it's not so amazing at all; the Slider, like Chancellor's Do Nothing worm, is imitating a darting baitfish rather than a worm. The Slider is typically fished on spinning tackle with 4 to 8 lb. line. It's great fun to fish and an excellent lure for both beginner and expert alike. Motor oil is a good color choice for the Slider worms; it will produce in very clear to dingy water.

Other Soft Plastic Lures: Grubs, twisters, lizards, and other soft plastic lures are designed to be fished by themselves on a jighead or as a trailer for spinnerbaits. These are extremely inexpensive lures and are good ones to experiment with. The *Sassy Shad,* a soft plastic minnow imitator, is an excellent lure. Fish these and other grub and corkscrew-type twisters on 1/16, 1/8, or 1/4 oz. jigheads; the hook may be left exposed or buried in the body of the lure. Productive colors for these lures include smoke, lime, white motor oil, and pearl.

Topwater Lures

Perhaps the most exciting bassin' occurs when a big bass slams a topwater plug. The ensuing boil in the water and frantic action is enough to make the heart of even the most jaded professional skip a beat! Thousands of different topwater variations are available. However, these can be divided into the following basic varieties:

Propeller Lures such as the Devil's Horse or Heddon Tiny Torpedo: Fish these by allowing the lure to rest a moment after casting it near a stump or other cover, then sweeping the lure forward with a brisk stroke of the rod. The propellers will sputter every time you repeat this action.

Poppers and Chuggers such as the Zara Spook or Burke Top Dog: One of the most difficult lures for the novice bass fisherman to master, the Zara (and similar stick lures) bobs to the surface after the cast, its head protruding above water at an angle. The fisherman sets the lure into a "walking" motion by twitching the rod tip and reeling at the same time. This lure has the capability of producing a tremendous amount of action in a limited area. Experts such as Missouri's Charlie Campbell can even make the lure walk backwards!

Wobblers such as the Jitterbug: These highly effective surface lures feature a curved metal plate at the head which causes the bait to wobble back and forth as it is reeled steadily along the surface. These lures are especially productive at night. Bass are attracted to the seductive action and steady blip-blip-blip sound of the wobbling lure.

Minnow Imitators such as the Rapala: These lifelike lures may be fished in a variety of ways, such as twitching the resting lure so that it darts in very small movements resembling the dying flutters of an injured minnow. Another way is simply casting and reeling, allowing the lure to swim in a lifelike manner; or by "rushing" the lure, allowing the lure to rest for a second or so, then sweeping the rod back sharply so that it rushes forward in a 3-to-5 ft. burst. Allowing the lure to rest between movements will send it floating slowly toward the surface.

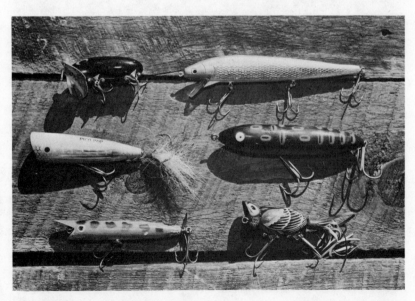

Topwater lures (clockwise from top left): Jitterbug, Rebel minnow, Zara Spook; Hula Popper, old Wood Mfg. Co. topwater plug, Pico Pop chugger.
Photo by Don Wirth

When and Where to Fish Topwater Lures: The preferred topwater seasons are during the warm months from mid to late spring into early fall. They are best fished in shallow water, around reeds and other cover, and in low light situations (early and late in the day). They are excellent choices for night fishing, especially the lures that produce a steady action such as the Jitterbug.

Basic Topwater Color Selection: You'll see hundreds of colors of topwater lures, but it's tough to top frog, chrome, and shad. A black lure is preferred for night fishing.

Crank Baits

This is a broad category of lures that gets its name from the fact that in order to achieve the desired action, the angler simply reels in (cranks) the bait. Crank baits often have a clear plastic lip which extends forward and causes the lure to dive and wobble upon retrieve. While thousands of types are available, we'll deal here with a few that have been proven by amateur and professional fishermen alike:

Crankbaits (clockwise from top left): Bagley Shad, Finn Mann, Deep Wee R, Hellbender, original Bomber, Model A Bomber.

Photo by Don Wirth

Rattlers (Rat-L-Trap, Hot Spot, Fin Mann): These thin-bodied lures sink quickly and vibrate upon retrieve, causing a rattling sound due to the metal shot inside the lures. A favored lure of the professional, the Rat-L-Trap's sloping head allows it to ride up over most obstructions. All of these lures sink at the rate of about 1 ft. per second, allowing you to "count down" the bait to the desired depth before reeling it in. Chrome is a great color for these lures as it causes them to resemble shad.

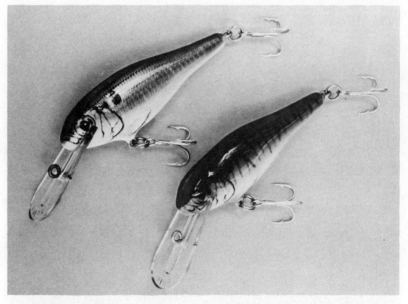

Deep-diving crankbaits such as these Bagley lures follow the contours of the bottom. They dive deeper on lighter line. Bagley photo

Deep Divers (Model A Bomber, Deep Wee R, Maxi R, Big O, Big N, Bagley Shad, etc.): These popular lures all feature a tear-drop-shaped body with a clear plastic lip. Most float at rest, then dive upon retrieve. The lighter the line used, the deeper they will dive. Excellent when fished over gravel points, bars, along stump rows, etc. They tend not to get hung up (except in weeds). These lures will virtually follow the contours of the bottom; just gradually speed up your retrieve as the bait gets further from the bank, and it will dive deeper. Shad, perch, crawfish, gold, and chrome are good color choices for these lures.

Crayfish Imitators (original Bomber, Hellbender, etc.): These are deep-diving, "bomb" shaped lures that are best fished right over the bottom; they'll climb and wobble over and around rocks, limbs, stumps, etc., and can crawl in and out of incredibly thick cover. They're excellent lures for trolling — the world record smallmouth bass was taken on a trolled Bomber. White, red and white, crayfish, and shad are good colors for these lures.

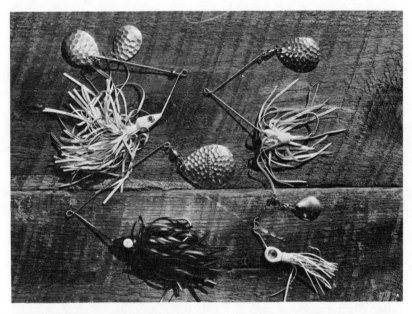

Spinnerbaits (clockwise from top left): Aggravator tandem spin, Jack's Dixie Spinner, Arbogast Spinner, Aggravator single spin.

Photo by Don Wirth

Spinnerbaits

The spinnerbait is perhaps the first artificial lure you should throw in the spring. It has the ability to excite sluggish bass in cold water. Also called the "safety pin" lure because of the bent wire framework supporting the blade over the hook, it can be fished in extremely heavy cover, including many weeds, and is virtually snag-free. The spinnerbait has a "dressing" of a plastic or rubber skirt around the hook, or a soft plastic trailer. It is often fished with a trailer hook attached to the primary hook, and with a pork frog. The Bushwacker, Aggravator, and H & H are three spinnerbaits we highly recommend. You will notice that spinnerbait blades come in a variety of shapes, sizes, and colors. We recommend a single or tandem spinner with small- to medium-size blades of either brass or nickel for starters. Brass is the preferred choice in murky water; nickel is best in clear water. The spinnerbait is a big fish lure, and many trophy bass have been taken on them. It may be fished in a variety of ways. The favorite method is to cast the lure close to cover and reel it in at a medium speed so that you can feel the blades vibrate. The lure also may be retrieved just under the surface so that the blades cause a wake; this is an excellent spring technique. *The spinnerbait is one of the very few lures that has any action while it's falling,* and many hits occur when anglers allow the lure to sink to the bottom. Fish the spinnerbait around grass, logjams, brushpiles, stickups, etc. A black spinnerbait is an excellent night lure.

Spinnerbaits and Buzz Baits (clockwise from top left): Zorro Aggravator tandem spinnerbait, Jack Chancellor "Half-Breed" spinner-buzz combination, Zorro Aggravator buzz bait.   Photo by Don Wirth

Buzz Baits

While basically an altered spinnerbait, the buzz bait is designed to run straight across the top of the water, over obstructions of almost any kind. It gets its name from the sputtering, buzzing sound it makes upon retrieve. Buzz baits have become extremely popular in recent years, and are very exciting and productive to fish. The buzz bait is one "topwater" lure you can fish effectively in the middle of the day in the summer — throw it around blowdowns, willow bushes, or sparse grass. It is often fished with a trailer hook. The authors' favorites include the Aggravator buzz bait, Floyd's, and Mann's Top Cat.

Straight Spinners

Often overlooked by Southern bass fishermen, but effective nonetheless, are the straight spinners such as the Mepps, Blue Fox Super Vibrax, and Rooster Tail. Most are not weedless, but all are great fish catchers, particularly in rivers. The smaller sizes are best fished on spinning gear with 6 or 8 lb. line.

Structure (Jigging) Spoons

These are heavy metal lures with a treble hook on one end, intended to be worked up and down (jigged) directly over the bottom, or in and around structure such as brushpiles, dropoffs, etc. They are especially effective in hot summer months when bass may be "holed up" — deeper fish tend to group together, and large numbers of big bass may be taken by the angler equipped with a spoon and the know-how to locate likely summer structure. A spoon is fished by merely flipping it over the side and allowing it to sink to the bottom, engaging the spool, and snapping the slack out of the line in a whipcrack fashion. This snap jerks the spoon off the bottom, causing it to flash and flutter like a dying shad. The lure should be "felt" back to the bottom by lowering the rod tip as the lure sinks. Never allow too much slack to get into the line because the bass will often hit the spoon as it falls, and the strike would not be detected. Good brands of spoons include Jack's Jigging Spoon, Hopkins, Red-Eye, and Krocodile. Jigging spoons are also good in the winter months when bass may be sluggish and located on steeply sloping banks; use smaller sizes in cold months.

Weighted Tailspinners

These are metal-bodied lures with a tailspinner, best typified by Mann's Little George and the Pedigo Spin-Rite. They are fished by casting out and allowing the lure to sink to the bottom, then sweeping back the rod tip sharply while reeling rapidly at the same time. The angler then stops reeling, the lure sinks, and the cycle is repeated. Many huge bass have been taken on these lures. They are best fished in relatively deep structure such as ledges, submerged roadbeds or brushpiles, etc. The lures also may be simply cast out and reeled in with a slow-to-medium, steady retrieve.

Thin Metal Vibrating Lures

These rather unusual-appearing lures represent a shad minnow to the bass. Most are unpainted metal or have a chrome finish. The most popular model is the Gay Blade. These lures are great for fishing schooling bass, especially early in the season when you need a smaller lure to match the shad. They may be cast a great distance, even in the wind. When retrieved quickly, they vibrate frantically. These lures are also excellent for fishing deep banks such as when fishing parallel to a steep bluff for smallmouth bass; they sink extremely fast and cover a lot of territory in a hurry.

Jigs (top): Round- and flat-headed jigheads; (middle): Flippin' jig with frog trailer; (bottom): 1/4 and 1/8 oz. hair jigs (Booza Flies).

Photo by Don Wirth

Jigs

The jig is one of the very best bass lures, and has increasingly become the choice of professional tournament anglers

who use the flipping technique, dropping the lure into extremely heavy cover on a very short, heavy line; the bass is
literally jerked from its hiding place into the boat (more on this
technique below). The jig is a very simple lure and will take
most species of fish. In bass fishing, the jig is usually a leadhead
lure of 1/8 to 5/8 oz. with hair or rubber covering the hook;
a soft plastic or cork trailer is usually applied.

Jigs and the Flipping Technique: Jigs have made a strong
emergence recently on the professional bass tournament trail,
thanks to a technique known as flipping. A collapsible rod of
approximately 7 feet is used, together with a level-wind baitcasting reel, and 20 to 30 lb. test line. The technique involves
the angler dropping or "flipping" the lure (usually a heavy,
weedless jig and trailer) directly into heavy cover on a short
line, rather than casting the lure as with other baits. By gently
raising and lowering the rod tip, the fisherman works the weedless jig in and around the root systems, tangled limbs, and heavy
weed growth where other lures cannot penetrate. He must
remain alert for the faintest tap signaling a bass has hit. When a
strike is detected, the fisherman rears back and slams home the
hook, usually pulling the bass upwards and immediately into
the boat, where it is then quickly deposited into the livewell.
While the sporting merits of flipping have been debated by
many, it is undeniably a highly successful technique, *particularly when bass are in a holding, not feeding, attitude.* It is
always best done from a boat, in the standing position. Because
there is usually little "play" to the fight, the bass have much
less chance to be overcome by stress and shock, and stand a
far better chance of being weighed in alive and released in
good shape following the tournament.

Other Types of Jigs: Smaller, less conspicuous jigs are
favored by anglers fishing the deep, clear highland reservoirs of
the mid-South, particularly in the colder months. The 1/8 to
1/4 oz. rubber or hair jig is the mainstay of the smallmouth bass
angler, when used with a pork or soft plastic trailer. The lure is
cast to a steep bank, allowed to settle, then lifted very slightly.
With the rod remaining in its highest position, the lure settles
again. On a steep bank, a small jig may be lifted only a couple
of inches, but falls several yards. *It is the perfect lure for the
smallmouth bass in winter months.* We highly recommend Stan
Sloan's Booza Bug and Booza Fly in the 1/8 to 1/4 oz. sizes.
Plain jigs of the same weight (without rubber or hair dressing)

may be substituted and used with soft plastic trailers. Smoke, lime, and motor oil are favorite colors in clear water; white and chartreuse in murky water. The Whistler is a unique jig incorporating a spinning propeller in front of the hook; as it falls or is ripped through the water, the prop flashes and emits a whistling sound. This lure is excellent for smallmouth bass, especially when fished on steeply sloping or bluff banks.

Weedless lures (clockwise from top left): Plummer's Superfrog, Johnson Silver Minnow with plastic corkscrew trailer, Dirty Bird, Zorro Booza Bug flipping jig with Mann's Auger Frog trailer, Burke Bassassin. Photo by Don Wirth

Weedless Lures

Weeds offer both great opportunity and great frustration to the bass angler. Most often, fishermen ignore the opportunity because of the frustration. But the use of several proven weedless lures will greatly increase your bass fishing pleasure and productivity. Here are the ones we recommend:

Johnson Silver Minnow is one of the true classic weedless lures. Fish it in and around weeds with a small plastic worm or pork trailer.

Buzz Baits may be fished effectively over and around many kinds of weeds, especially grasses.

Snagless Sally is great when fished around lilypads.

Bill Plummer's Superfrog is a great big bass lure; fish it around weeds, shorelines, and boat docks.

Weed Wing's sputtering, fluttering action has taken many a weed-bound bass.

Dirty Bird is extremely effective when cast 6 feet or so into the weeds, then worked over the edge, allowing the lure to sink when it hits clear water. The bright, metallic bill flashes as the lure falls; many hits occur as it enters open water.

Weedless Plugs are the latest development for fishing weeds and the new soft-bodied "Weed Beater" lures by Burke can be fished anywhere.

Plastic Worms rigged with no sinkers and weedless hooks are excellent weedless lures that may be thrown far back into the weed growth and retrieved over the edge.

Flipping Baits (heavy jigs with trailers and pegged plastic worms) are excellent producers of big bass buried thick in the weed growth; a powerful flipping rod is necessary to fish them.

Jigging Spoons, while certainly not weedless, are highly effective when fished right at the edges of weedbeds, especially hyacinths. Bass holding in the weeds will rush out into clear water to strike a spoon.

Weed Fishing Tips:

(1) Use a long rod. By holding the rod in the one o'clock position when retrieving lures through weeds, more line is lifted clear of the weeds and tangles are avoided.

(2) Be alert for surface activity. Bream popping, bass boiling or moving are all signs that feeding is taking place. Cast to one side or beyond a feeding bass, not directly to a boil.

(3) Use stout tackle. Many bass, when hooked, bury themselves deep in the weeds; you may find it easier to go in after the fish than to try to reel the fish back to you.

Matching Your Tackle to Your Lure

The professional golfer doesn't attempt to traverse 18 holes with only a driver; neither does the professional angler attempt to fish a tournament with one rod and reel. Specialized tackle has evolved, and while you may limit yourself to only one or two bass outfits for starters, as your interest and ability grow, so will your tackle collection. Remember that if you have a strong preference, either baitcasting, spinning, or spincast equipment can be used for almost any situation. The following are the types of rods and reels that will allow you to most effectively fish a given type of lure:

Crank Baits and Metal Vibrating Lures: A medium-action rod and baitcasting reel with 12 to 14 lb. line will allow you some degree of casting distance plus enough backbone to handle a heavy fish. Strong hook-setting ability is not that necessary because of the lures' treble hooks. Rods up to and slightly over 6 feet are popular for this application.

Spinnerbaits and Buzz Baits: Use a fiberglass rod with some degree of give as opposed to the stiffer boron or graphite rod, with a baitcasting reel and 14 to 17 lb. line.

Plastic Worms: A stout fiberglass or boron rod around 6 feet with a fast tip, plus a baitcasting or spincast reel, and 14 to 20 lb. line.

Do Nothing Worm Rig: A stiff, long-handled casting rod over 6 feet is necessary to avoid hooking yourself while casting.

Topwater Lures: Use a medium-action baitcasting rod with 10 to 14 lb. line.

Small Jigs and Spinners: Use any well-balanced spinning or spincast rig; the fiberglass Slider rod with a light spinning reel, and 6 to 8 lb. test can't be beat.

Flipping Jigs: Use a long, collapsible flipping rod with a baitcasting reel, and 20 to 30 lb. line or saltwater spinning tackle.

Weedless Lures: Use a long, powerful rod (a flipping rod may be utilized) with a baitcasting reel, and 14 to 20 lb. line.

Structure Spoons and Metal Tailspinners: Use a stout fiberglass or boron rod with a fast tip; a baitcasting reel with 14 to 20 lb. line.

Is Lure Color Important?

Many anglers try to accumulate every color of every type lure they use. This is distracting and time-consuming when on the water as the angler is presenting himself with too many choices. In general, *it's more important that a lure contrast with its environment and is visible than to exactly imitate a certain type of baitfish or other prey.* Look for lures that project a generalized appearance to the bass. One lure with a silver side is sufficient, rather than six different shad imitations that may represent the varying hues of the baitfish. Stay very general in your color selections. You do not need one of every color!

Bass hit lures because of their general form and movement, not because they imitate their prey exactly.

What Lure Colors Should I Choose?

Your tacklebox need not be the size of a Crosley station wagon! Pick up a few of the lures listed below and you'll catch bass.

Crank Baits — brown and orange (crayfish), shad or perch, "baby bass."

Topwater Plugs — frog, perch or shad, chrome.

Plastic Worms — purple, "electric grape," black, motor oil, blue.

Spinnerbaits — white, black/chartreuse, blue/white, black.

Buzz Baits — white, blue/white, chartreuse.

Straight Spinners — gold, silver, black.

Vibrating Lures — shad, chartreuse, chrome.

Flipping Jigs — brown, black, brown/orange.

Smaller Jigs — brown, brown/orange, chartreuse, yellow, white.

Minnow Imitators — gold, shad, chrome.

Weedless Lures — frog, chrome, black.

Do Nothing Worms — red, chartreuse, smoke.

Jigging Spoons, Metal Vibrating Lures, Tailspinners — chrome.

A glance through the above recommendations will tell you that certain colors work best in certain classes of lures. For example, brown/orange lures represent crayfish to the bass; *you don't need a brown/orange topwater plug because crayfish swim on the bottom.* Similarly, crankbaits follow the bottom contours where crayfish lurk; *you don't need a frog-pattern crankbait.* As a general rule, use the following strata or depth ranges as a guide in selecting lure colors:

Top — frog, shad, chrome.

Mid-range — shad, perch, "baby bass."

Bottom — crayfish, purple, black (worms); white (spinnerbaits); chrome (spoons, metal vibrators, tailspinners).

Weeds — all of the above.

CHAPTER

4

Live Bait Fishing

THE USE of live bait in bass fishing is one of the oldest and most traditional methods of catching bass; the largest bass are sometimes taken with live bait. This is because a lure, such as a crankbait, presents many cues to a bass which it can eventually learn to reject (wobbling, rattling, etc.). A huge bass may be hooked and escape many times during its lifespan and can learn to reject certain offerings. *A live bait such as a shad, crayfish, or frog, on the other hand, presents only natural cues to the bass.* Live bait fishing has received much criticism among modern-day bass anglers, who often condemn it simply because it is prohibited in bass tournaments. The fact that lure manufacturers sponsor most top-name professionals makes such criticism understandable. However, we highly recommend that the angler try live bait fishing before forming an opinion of it. We believe the use of live bait has advantages that are simply unattainable in other kinds of fishing, mainly: (1) It is extremely relaxing and allows you to fish with an easy pace, letting you sit back and enjoy your surroundings while still participating in bass fishing; (2) It is highly productive when properly executed — the authors have taken many bass over 10 lbs. on live bait; (3) It is highly exciting — the sight of a huge bass boiling in pursuit of a trolled wild shiner, for example, is unparalleled in the basser's world; (4) Live bait lets you work a small area for a long period of time, a great advantage when bass are moody; (5) Live bait may be caught and used by the fishermen with no money investment, as opposed to the necessity of purchasing other types of bait; (6) Live bait is the "natural" way to fish; many anglers may appreciate the sense that this is how their grandfathers or ancestors fished.

Types of Live Bait for Bass

As we have seen, bass are a highly generalized fish and will eat a wide variety of prey: shiners, bluegills, minnows, worms, crayfish, frogs, salamanders, eels, trout, even mice and birds. But rather than have you scour the woods for mice and birds, we'll deal here with the more popular forms of live bait for bass and how to fish them.

Wild Shiners: In the big bass waters of mid-Florida and elsewhere, it's tough to beat a large, wild shiner as a bass bait. Wild shiners are highly preferred over "store-bought" shiners; breeding in hatcheries and tanks literally breeds the fear instinct right out of the bait! The bass not only react to a wild shiner as food but are aroused by its flight behavior. A wild shiner, when it sees a bass, almost radiates fear; the bass senses this and attacks the prey with a vengeance. You can catch wild shiners on a light spinning rig with a small hook and oatmeal or breadballs as bait. Simply chum some bait out until the shiners begin to gather and cast the baited hook in their midst. At $8 to $10 a dozen, catching your own wild shiners makes sense. It is especially fun for children, too.

Author Don Wirth wrestles aboard a big bass that he hooked on a wild shiner. Live bait-fishing has received much undue criticism in recent years, but it offers unparalleled excitement.

Photo by Doug Hannon

Wild shiners may be fished in several ways. *Cork fishing or still fishing* is the preferred way of fishing most live baits, including shiners. Free-lining the bait into deep holes in lakes and rivers is one of the most effective ways of fishing live bait. However, a shiner or other bait can be floated up to the edge of heavy cover or vegetation under a cork or even free-lined under floating mats of weeds with good results. When using a cork it is to your advantage for the line to float between you and the cork to avoid tangling on the bottom. Many line dressings are available; we recommend the use of a floating line such as "squidding line" or even one of the good floating fly lines instead. These braided lines are highly visible. The angler should attach a 3-foot section of monofilament line to them as an invisible leader.

When cork fishing with shiners, hook the bait on a weedless hook through the lips or behind the dorsal fin. Rig a cork or stick bobber, not the plastic pushbutton kind, 3 feet above the bait, allowing the shiner to swim about. When a bass approaches, you will notice the shiner frantically rolling, leaping, and tugging at the line in its efforts to escape. The bass may also be visible, rolling and boiling about. When the bass finally takes the shiner, set the hook as quickly as possible using the slack-line technique described in the plastic worm section of Chapter Three. *Do not let the bass run with the bait.* It is imperative that the angler not hit the bass on a tight line; this will merely turn the head of a big fish and will cause it to blow out the bait. How long to wait before setting the hook is a matter of much controversy in bass fishing circles, but our studies and angling experience have proven that a feeding bass will immediately inhale the entire shiner. At best, waiting too long will result in a missed fish; at worst, the fish will be gut-hooked and would be likely to die if the angler should choose to release it. For shiner fishing, use the Eagle Claw #84-RP hook from 3/0 to 5/0, depending on the size of the bait. Don't shy away from huge "mule ear" shiners around a foot long; they are excellent baits for huge bass. We have taken fish in the 17 lb. range on such shiners.

Trolling large wild shiners can be a good alternative to cork fishing. With the electric trolling motor set on medium or the small gasoline motor barely above idle speed, let out about 100 ft. of line with a shiner hooked through both lips on a weedless hook. Troll the bait along weedy shorelines, hyacinth beds, and other likely habitat. Be alert for frantic movements of the shiner — these signal the approach of a bass. Utilize the slack-line hookset when hitting the fish. Avoid cutting the motor on and off during the course of your trolling; we have found that bassin' is more productive, particularly in shallow, remote waters, when the motor is allowed to remain on constantly. The bass seem to adjust more to a constant sound than to an on-off sound.

Drifting is another excellent method of fishing wild shiners and other types of live bait, and is especially productive in more open waters, such as over a weed bed in the middle of the lake, in the mouth of a large cove, etc. Using no weight or corks, the bait is simply allowed to swim freely as the boat moves with the wind or current. A drawback of this method is that shiners and other natural baits often head for cover and get hung up in weeds, grasses, or rocks.

Minnows: Many huge bass have been taken by crappie or perch fishermen using minnows on a cane pole. Minnows may be fished off the bottom using a split shot or two placed 18 inches above the bait, on bobbers, or by drifting. Hook small minnows through the lips or behind the dorsal fin.

Crayfish: Crayfish are easily collected under rocks or debris in shallow streams, or by lowering a piece of bacon tied to your line around a boat dock; very carefully lift the crayfish from the water when it grabs the bacon. The crayfish is an excellent natural bait in the deep, clear reservoirs and lakes with rock and gravel bottoms, and is the preferred food of the smallmouth bass. Hook the crayfish in the tail, placing one or two split shots above the bait about 18 inches, and allow it to crawl along the bottom. Let a bass run about 5 seconds with the bait when you detect a strike, then set the hook. Crayfish will attempt to crawl under rocks and debris and frequently hang up, but they are often worth the hassles involved in fishing them.

Salamanders: Salamanders, or "spring lizards," have a maximum amount of wiggle! Find them in small creeks or run-offs under rocks and leaves; they are exceedingly slimy and hard to handle. Before hooking, grasp the lizard in the palm of your hand and roll it gently on your pant leg — this will remove the slime and make the critter easier to handle. Trying to hook a wet, writhing salamander is like squeezing a bar of soap; it tends to shoot out of your grasp and escape! Use a small gold or black wire hook and force the hook up through the lower jaw, out the gristle on the top of its head. We have had the best success using the 3 to 4 inch black or brown salamanders, as opposed to the larger, more brightly colored specimens. Brightly colored amphibians such as the tiger salamander have these loud colors as a warning to tell predators of their bad-tasting mucus coating. In the same way that you would not pick up a bumble bee or a coral snake, the bass will usually leave these gaudy creatures alone.

The salamander may be cast out to steeply sloping or bluff banks and allowed to swim freely, or a split shot may be used above the lure a foot or so. The bait may also be fished effectively as a trailer on a 1/8 or 1/4 oz. jig. A live salamander, fished in this manner on a spinning rig with 6 or 8 lb. line, is one of the very best baits for huge smallmouth bass in the spring.

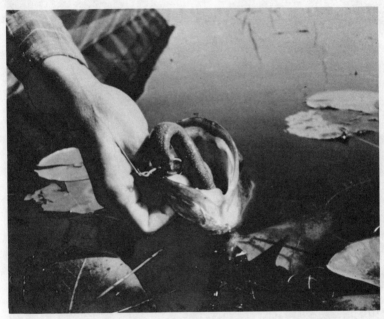

The Florida state record bass was caught on a live eel like the one shown above.

Other Live Baits: Bass will eat just about anything that enters the water. Fish frogs by hooking them through the leg or lips with a weedless hook. Nightcrawlers may be fished with a spinner harness, with a split shot, or simply in a glob on a wire hook.

Live bait is fun to experiment with and costs nothing to use if the angler gathers it himself. As a rule of thumb, fish live bait no faster than the natural swimming action of the bait you're using. Generally, slower is better if the bait is to be moved at all. Some huge bass have been taken, many of them by fishermen standing on the bank, using live bait. Who knows? The next world record bass may well be taken on live bait. Give it a try; it may become your favorite kind of fishing!

Now is the time to put the pieces of the puzzle together and catch bass like this.

Catching Bass
in All Four Seasons

NOW IS THE TIME for the beginning bass fisherman to put the
pieces of the puzzle together. It might be helpful at this point
to reread Chapter One. A general understanding of the bass and
its world will go a long, long way toward making you a successful bass angler!

As we have seen, bass are to be found in different places at
different times of the year. This is because they are cold-
blooded creatures whose body temperature (and therefore,
metabolism) is in a direct relationship with their surroundings.
To find bass in the varying seasons does not require a boat, a
depth finder, a pH meter, a surface temperature gauge, or other
specialized equipment, although some or all of it might make
the task easier. *Using your eyes and general awareness of bass
behavior, you can find — and catch — bass, no matter the time
of year.*

Spring Bassin'

It's the spawning season. Fish will be in shallow water and
will be very aggressive. They will take virtually any artificial or
natural bait at this time. In general, lures that can be worked
faster (crankbaits and spinnerbaits as opposed to plastic worms
or jigs) will enable you to cover more water and catch more bass
in the spring. Start fishing in the northwest sections of the lake.
Look for blooming weed beds; these will exhibit a vibrant green
color in clear water, similar to the intense chartreuse color of
new leaves on trees. Blooming weeds produce maximum oxygen
and attract more life forms. Check the mouths of coves with
deep-diving crankbaits when the surface temperature gets into
the high 50s. Seek out the warmest water you can find in the
spring; a simple outdoor thermometer on a line will supply you
with temperature information.

Manmade canals are excellent places for spring bassin'. Always try the back of the canal first. Saddles or high spots in slow-moving rivers are excellent spawning places. In rivers with more current, fish the widest, slowest-moving sections using the baits described. Be advised that spring fishing is often characterized by multiple frontal passages, high, muddy water, and high winds, making bassin' difficult. Always try to fish on the new (dark) moon in the spring as the bass tend to concentrate their feeding activity around this moon phase; they tend to use the full moon as a clock to time their spawning.

Spring is the season to catch giant bass in shallow waters.

Summer Bassin'

In a shallow lake (20 ft. or less), fish will seek the flats (areas where the water depth every 50 ft. does not drop more than 5 ft.). The biggest, weediest or brushiest flats are the very best in the summer. The bass are more sluggish than in the spring and cannot expend as much energy. A plastic worm is a good lure in the summer, for it moves slowly and may be easily inhaled by a bass sulking on the bottom. Prey that travel in large schools are sought, such as threadfin shad. Bass will gather in groups and ravage these schools in short, violent bursts; often acres of bass may be seen wildly feeding on shad, only to suddenly disappear as they stop to conserve their metabolic activity. Almost any topwater lure will take them during these "schooling" periods; chrome lures are excellent. The Rat-L-Trap and Little George are fine schooling bass lures.

In the summer, expect to catch bass in intermediate depths (6 to 8 ft.) on flats, but don't ignore deeper structure. In man-made reservoirs, a boat can take you to ledges where the old river channel winds through the lake. A depth finder is helpful in locating these; however, you can also line up with channel marker buoys fairly easily. Prime depths here are 15 to 25 ft.; bass will often hold at the edge of the shallow and deep areas and may be taken with plastic worms, Do Nothing worm rigs, large deep-diving crankbaits such as the Maxi-R, or jigging spoons. Night fishing is best in the summer. Plastic worms, large jigs, and topwater lures are favored; black is a key color. A steady retrieve is best at night, for it allows bass to see and track your lure more easily.

Rivers may be better than lakes for summer bassin', particularly for the angler lacking a bass boat and a lot of electronic gear. Rivers are typically cooler than lakes in the summer and the bass, therefore, are more aggressive. The Do Nothing rig and the jigging spoon are two fantastic lures for summer bass in rivers. Seek out high spots, bends, and eddies. *Fish don't fight current, they avoid it.* Look for bass behind logs, rocks, pilings, or anywhere the flow of the current is diverted. Learning how to read the current is the key to successful river fishing. Oxbows are good bassin' spots at this time; the current is vastly reduced. The world record largemouth was taken in an oxbow during the summer. Be aware of power generation schedules in tailwaters of reservoirs, for increased current generally means a pickup in fish activity. Fish will move on top of structure at these times —

fish mounds, sandbars, and ledges in water shallower than during periods of no flow. *Always exercise extreme caution when fishing below a power dam as the current may be dangerously heavy.*

Summer bass are often located "in the middle of the lake" on large brushy flats, creek channels, and other structure where the opportunity for maximum food intake with the minimum energy expenditure is afforded the bass. Here expert angler Rex Riley of Eufaula, Alabama, fishes a plastic worm on a ledge at famed Lake Eufaula.

Photo by Hobby Morrison

Fall Bassin'

In a lake the fall is often the very best time to fish for a couple of reasons: the water has cooled down and the fish are more aggressive, and you may have the lake to yourself once the television football season starts! In general, fish will move off the flats and summer holding structures and seek out the points, edges of flats, and the last green weeds. The bass position themselves closer to deeper water as a protection against approaching cold frontal passages. *Fall is a great time to troll.* The bass will be more highly mobile during the fall than at any other time of year; covering a lot of ground is to your advantage. Seek out isolated cover such as a lone bush at the end of a long point. Because baitfish have had all summer to grow up, you should use larger lures such as the big Bombers, Hellbenders, or

Maxi-Rs at this time. Crayfish become prevalent in many lakes in the fall; crankbaits with orange in them are excellent choices as the bass begin feeding heavily on crayfish, their shad forage having scattered.

In a river seek out the areas closest to the sloughs and flats in slightly deeper water, as well as along the shoreline. Try spoons, jigs, and Do Nothing worms for best results.

Winter Bassin'

The metabolism of the bass slows down enormously in cold water. In 50-degree water it may take 12 times as long for the bass to digest its food as in 80-degree water; hence, *cold-water bass feed very little and prefer small morsels when they do.* Seek out steeply sloping banks which permit the bass to move from deep to shallower water by expending a minimum of effort. The small jig and pork rind combination is the best choice in the winter. Fish it right on the bottom, gently lifting the bait and allowing it to drop from ledge to ledge. Other lure choices would be a jigging spoon fished right over the bottom, metal vibrating lures such as the Gay Blade, and weighted tail-spinners including the Little George and Pedigo Spinrite. All of these present a relatively small mass to the fish and may be worked slowly just over the bottom on deeper water.

In the winter a river is often a better place to fish than a lake. Rivers tend to stay slightly warmer than do lakes, although the fish will also be less active in rivers during the winter than in the warmer months. Fish the ends of deep pools or holes where the river gets narrower and runs deeper. Use light-colored jigs, small spinners such as the Blue Fox Super Vibrax, and tail-spinners. Fish small lures that can be "swept away" in the current in a more natural manner to tempt a sluggish bigmouth.

Summing Up:
Change as the Bass Change

As a rule, bass won't be in the same places at different times of the year. As the bass change their movements and habits, so must the successful angler change his lures and presentations. However, it is also true that the bass is not a migratory fish such as the salmon or walleye; bass seldom move a tremendous distance — often only a few hundred yards or less. *Therefore, the very best bass fishing is usually found where spring, summer, fall, and winter habitats may occur closest together.* A locale with shallow areas, flats, ledges, and steep sloping banks — all within close proximity — can hold the key to the best bass fishing in that body of water. While your tendency may be to return time and again to those places where bass were taken previously, fishing a shallow stump where a 7-pounder was taken in the spring will probably be fruitless in the winter. Use your knowledge of bass behavior to key you in to the places bass are most likely to be found at a given time of year.

CHAPTER

6

Boats and Bassin'

YOU MAY never need a boat, especially if you limit your fishing to small ponds, many rivers, or even the shallow areas of some lakes. Many huge bass have been caught by anglers wading or bank fishing. If you fish only a couple of times a year, a boat for bass fishing alone is a questionable purchase; rental boats are usually available at marinas, equipped with small outboard engines. One of the very best things you can buy, even if you do not own nor intend to purchase a boat, is an electric trolling motor, together with a powerful deep-cycle battery of 80 amps or more. Bass are object-related fish as we have seen, and to fish these objects (weedbeds, stump rows, brushpiles, etc.) in an effective manner requires that you maintain your boat's position. This is most easily accomplished with an electric trolling motor. We advise purchasing a 12-volt, clamp-on motor that may be operated from either the stern, bow or gunwale of the boat; you may have to rotate the motor's head depending on where you mount it, but it's a simple procedure involving drilling a couple of new holes in the top of the shaft. A trolling motor equipped with a weedless prop such as the Motor Guide is an excellent choice; most trolling motor props are *not* weedless and your motor may fail to function and perhaps be seriously damaged if you attempt to operate it in heavy weeds. Weed cages are available for non-weedless props; they can be of some help if the weeds aren't too thick.

Match the Boat to the Water

When selecting a bass fishing boat, the first rule of thumb is to get the right kind of boat for the places you'll be fishing. If you're a pond fisherman, you won't want to consider a 17-ft. bass boat with a powerful V-6 outboard; the inexpensive "bassin' platforms" may be perfect for you, as may a 10 to 14 ft. jon boat. Obviously, if you are intent on fishing a huge reservoir, you'll want a bigger, safer craft with a more powerful motor to take you to farflung places and carry you safely back to the ramp should a sudden storm occur. If you are fishing smaller, natural lakes and rivers with marginal launching facilities, it's tough to beat a 14-ft. aluminum jon boat; these are relatively inexpensive and have the ability to sneak into out-of-the-way places where the lunkers lurk.

A low-sided aluminum flatbottom boat is perfect for fishing remote areas where big bass lurk. Here author Don Wirth wrestles a big bass into the boat. Note camouflaged clothing, boat — it pays to fit in, not stick out, where bassin' is concerned.

Photo by Doug Hannon

Match the Boat to Your Needs

If you want to do nothing but fish, a regular bass boat may be perfect; if you want to go waterskiing and cruising the lake with the family as well as fishing, a bass boat's seating configuration may not be ideal for you. "Fish 'n Ski" models are available which offer the compromise of bass boat maneuverability with a trolling motor on the bow, as well as skiing and cruising seating comfort. If you are intent on joining a bass club and fishing tournaments on very large lakes, a small aluminum boat may not fulfill your needs; you may find you spend all your time running and little time actually fishing. If you "need" to have a sharp-looking, high-performance bass boat to be the envy of your buddies, even a more expensive, fully-equipped aluminum bass boat won't make you happy in the long run. As a rule, it's better to wait until you can afford what you really want when you are thinking about making a boating purchase. Many excellent buys are available in used bass boats, and it pays to shop the want ads carefully. Often a late-model, fully-equipped bass boat can be purchased for thousands of dollars less than can a new one.

Fiberglass Bass Boats

Today's high-speed, low-profile, fiberglass bass boats are a marvel of efficiency. Modern hull designs permit the boat to lift up over the surface of the water, riding on only a very small area (the "pad"), thereby providing a Cadillac-smooth ride with minimum gas consumption and maximum speed. Many novice bassers have been attracted to the sport not by the bass, but by the sleek, fast boats, many of which exceed speeds of 70 mph. These boats are best suited to the sprawling impoundments where the water can get rough in a hurry and the bass habitat may be farflung. The newcomer may certainly find fishing from one of these "bassin' machines" far more pleasurable than from a back-breaking rental rowboat; however, we advise that you examine your needs closely before making an investment of $10,000 or more in a boat such as this. You'll need a tow vehicle powerful enough to haul a big boat; today's 4-cylinder vehicles may not do the job. If you are intent on buying a high-performance bass boat, here are a few points to remember:

1. Buy from a large, reputable manufacturer who has been in business a while and intends to stay in business. Many "mom and pop" boat companies appear on the scene from time to time; avoid these because they may not be around to handle warranty claims.
2. Select a boat on hull design and construction, not upon cosmetic gimmickry. The best construction material currently available is Kevlar, a material used in bullet-proof vests and resembling fiberglass cloth but far stronger. A Kevlar hull is more expensive but the investment may be worth it if you intend to keep the boat any length of time. Hydra-Sports pioneered Kev-

lar hull construction in bass boats; today it is available in several brands. A boat with a Kevlar hull is almost always manufactured using hand-laid construction, which is superior to other construction techniques.

Kevlar, a high-tech fiber, is the strongest material currently available for bass boat hulls, as this dramatic demonstration proves. The Hydra-Sports bass boat with Kevlar hull was undamaged by the "Cat."
Photo by Hydra-Sports

3. Never overpower your boat, and don't think you have to use the maximum rated outboard to get adequate performance. The best bass boat manufacturers today indicate a horsepower range under which a given hull is designed to perform — for example, a 17 ft., 3 in. bass boat may have a suggested horsepower range of 115 to 150, with 150 being the maximum Coast Guard rating. While this boat will obviously run faster with a 150, you can use a 115 and enjoy the hull you paid for; using a smaller motor such as a 70 will rob you of the true potential of the hull.

4. Never operate your boat without a safety cut-off device ("kill switch") attached to your person.

5. Avoid getting caught up in high performance gadgetry such as streamlined lower units, exotic propellers, and other racing components. A given stock boat and motor combination has a certain top-speed range; going beyond that range will cost you approximately $500 for every one mile per hour, not to mention your time and trouble. Manufacturers today have

plenty of performance built into their standard hulls, engines, and props.

6. The propeller you select will have a tremendous bearing on your boat's performance, and ultimately your boating satisfaction. Propellers that make your boat run at the fastest top-end speed also tend to make your boat slowest to get up on plane. Ask the manufacturer or dealer which prop he recommends for the best *all-around* bass fishing performance: a good "hole shot" (plane-off), good mid-range performance, and good top-end speed.

7. Select a boat dealer not only by his asking price but by his service department.

8. Insist on all warranties and guarantees in writing. Reputable dealers and manufacturers will gladly honor any warranty repair work.

9. *Don't let the boat become more important than the bass.* Today's avid bassers are finding that using boats with stock set-ups and equipment, as opposed to endless fine-tuning of their bass rigs, has resulted in more bass being caught and less headaches.

10. Select a quality bass boat trailer that will offer excellent support of your boat. The majority of insurance liability claims involving boats are a result of trailering accidents, not on-the-water accidents. Things to look for in a trailer: 14-inch or larger wheels, proper placement of rails, grease fittings allowing you to pack the wheel bearings with a grease gun, safety chains, and a spare wheel and tire. Don't skimp on your boat trailer; a good trailer may retail for as much as $1,500. A quality trailer is essential to carry your boat safely at highway speeds.

11. Power trim is of great benefit on a bass boat; you can't get the full benefit of a high-performance hull without it. It's also excellent for all kinds of fishing boats in shallow water. Power trim enables you to change the angle of the propeller with a switch (usually located on the throttle). Trimming the engine UP changes the angle of the prop and serves to lift the boat into its most efficient operating attitude. Trimming the engine IN brings the bow down.

12. Insist on a working tachometer in a bass boat. The tach registers the revolutions per minute of the prop and serves to monitor the "heartbeat" of your engine. A tach is far more important than a marine speedometer, which is usually inaccurate. The tach will tell you whether or not you are operating your engine within its recommended range, whether your engine is malfunctioning, etc.

Aluminum Bass Boats

For thousands of bassers, the modern aluminum flatbottom bass boats such as the Fisher Marine, Bass Pro Shops' Bass Tracker, Alumacraft, and others have proven a valuable asset. If you fish smaller lakes or rivers where high speeds and rough-water stability are not as important as ease of maneuverability, one of these economical aluminum bass boats may be the answer. They are typically at home in shallow, weedy lakes or rivers. They require virtually no maintenance and are extremely durable. One of the primary benefits of aluminum bass boats is their ability to be towed by lighter vehicles, thus cutting your operating expenses. Aluminum boats are more easily launched in secondary fishing situations such as where no ramps may exist; the combination of a four-wheel drive tow vehicle and an aluminum bass boat is tough to beat when backwoods bassin' is what turns you on. Always stay well within the maximum horsepower rating of an aluminum boat; overpowering makes its handling unstable and may cause the hull to buckle. Even a flat-bottom jon boat purchased from a discount store may be turned into a "bass boat" by the handy fisherman; the addition of swivel seats, a trolling motor, and a removable ice chest with an aerator pump will certainly make your inexpensive purchase more pleasurable and efficient to use.

A fully-rigged aluminum bass boat such as this Bass Tracker offers economy of operation and great maneuverability.

Bass Pro Shops photo

Bass Boating Tips

The beginning boater/basser should be aware that there are several do's and dont's that can help him catch more fish and enjoy time spent on the water more. Among these are:

1. Always obey the "rules of the water" and never speed in a No Wake zone, mix alcohol with boating, etc.

2. Give other fishermen and pleasure boaters wide berth. Nothing tees off another fisherman more than having a boat run between him and the bank he's fishing, or seeing another boat pull up and its occupants begin fishing an area he's trying to work.

3. Always wear a life jacket when the big engine is in operation. Insist on a high-quality personal flotation device for you and every person aboard. Make sure all Coast Guard required safety equipment is on board and operational.

4. Always tell someone where you'll be fishing and when you plan to return.

5. Even though it may appear "professional," avoid standing up to fish, especially in clear water. When a good bass is hooked, don't stand up to watch the fight. The fish will see you and attempt to run under the boat, jump, etc. Many big bass are lost when they panic upon seeing a standing angler.

6. Insist on an operational aerated livewell system when purchasing a bass boat, or construct your own from a large cooler and an aerator pump. Properly aerated bass mean more points to the tournament angler, and fish stand a good chance of surviving following release if maintained in a livewell.

Electronic Equipment

The modern bass boat resembles a sophisticated jet fighter with its staggering array of electronic gadgetry, devices designed to measure most every aspect of the bass' world. As exciting and alluring as it may seem, electronic gear is expensive, too; the full complement of bassin' electronics may add another $5,000 to the already high price of a boat, motor, and trailer. Much of this electronic gear is better suited to the huge reservoir than to the small lake, as it can help the angler determine recurring conditions in farflung places in a hurry.

Basic Electronic Gear: Besides a trolling motor, perhaps the most important electronic tool a fisherman can learn to use correctly is a flasher depth sounder, or "fish finder" as they are popularly (if somewhat inaccurately) known. We recommend purchasing one of the major brands such as a Lowrance, Hum-

min-bird, or Eagle. These are sonar devices with a transducer
which sends a signal to the bottom and reads it as it bounces
back to the boat. While they can, indeed, show fish (as light
blips), their primary purpose is to help you read the contours
of the bottom of the lake; when you know that there are
objects or "edges" down there, bass are most likely to be found.
A depth sounder can answer many questions about the bottom,
such as: Is the bottom flat, or does it slope sharply? Is there
cover on the bottom such as brush, stumps or trees? To read
the depth sounder, one must thoroughly acquaint himself with
the unit's operating manual; few bass fishermen ever become
totally adept at deciphering all of the information presented on
the flasher in the form of light blips. The fisherman with no
boat may consider the purchase of a portable flasher unit which
may be moved from craft to craft — it may even be used
through the ice. Follow all instructions as to proper placement
of the transducer. If problems develop, use the toll-free service
line provided by most of the major manufacturers.

A few of the many electronic devices available for bass fishing: the large
device at top left is a chart recorder; the "boxes" are electronic flasher
units of various models. A portable flasher is at top right. At the bottom:
a surface temperature meter (left) and a compact in-dash depth finder
flasher unit (right).
                                                              Techsonic photo

Chart Recorders: Chart recorders or "graphs" are sophisticated electronic tools which, instead of indicating the depth through light flashes, literally draw or televise a picture of everything between you and the bottom. They operate using paper or, in the most expensive versions, video screens. While they can reveal an incredible amount of information about the bottom and the water, *the novice angler is often incapable of putting all this information to use.* We recommend that the beginner start with the less expensive flasher unit; a chart recorder may be considered in the future. Graphs may utilize microcomputers and LCD displays. Graphs are more delicate than flashers and must be handled with care — most serious anglers remove them from their boats during trailering to avoid too much vibration. In the hands of a knowledgeable angler, few tools are better suited to bass fishing than a chart recorder. It will print out individual fish, groups of fish, even thermoclines. It will not tell you whether a fish printed on the paper is a carp or a bass; your knowledge of bass behavior can help you determine this from its position and proximity to structure.

Surface Temperature Gauges: The surface temperature gauge features an external thermometer which mounts on your boat, and is sometimes a feature included in some premium-priced depth sounders as opposed to a separate unit. The meter delivers the temperature information, often in LCD form. This is important input when you recall that water temperature is a direct measure of the metabolism of fish. It is especially useful in the spring, as the warmest water is sure to attract fish.

These are only a few of the electronic gadgets available to the bass fisherman, but they are the ones we feel are especially important for the novice to understand. As a rule of thumb, we'd list the flasher-type depth sounder as the one to have; as your bass fishing knowledge and needs grow, so will your equipment.

Summing Up:
Boats and Bassin'

Remember, don't let the boat become the primary focus of the sport. Choose a functional boat that does the job in an efficient manner. In boating, as in other hobbies such as photography, your accumulation of equipment tends to grow as does your interest and proficiency; there are beginner's camera kits just as there are simple boats and motors, and there are high-priced photographic systems just as there are top-dollar bass rigs with all the gear imaginable. *For the beginning angler, no priority is more important than simplicity and utility when considering the purchase of a boat.*

A bass boat's trailer must offer proper support and safety while trailering. Note the double bunks on this Custom Frames trailer; it's perfectly matched to the hull of this Hydra-Sports bass boat. Photo by Don Wirth

Golden Opportunities

SOME BASS FISHING situations present unusual opportunities for the alert angler to catch lots of fish, and/or especially big fish. True, you may "luck into" finding one or more of these situations, but you can find that your "luck" improves greatly when you know what you are looking for. We'll briefly outline especially good situations you should be aware of, situations that are very conducive to bass fishing success.

Schooling Bass

Bass are not "school fish" as are walleye or crappie; at times, however, they gather as a group of individuals when unusually good feeding opportunities exist. Typically in Southern reservoirs, these opportunities center around vast schools of threadfin shad. During hot weather, the bass must be careful not to exert itself too much — remember, its metabolic rate has increased vastly due to the increased water temperature. Groups of bass tend to position themselves on brushy flats or on the edges of dropoffs, holding there until the food comes to them. When a school of shad enters the area, these bass will hunt them down in much the same way a pack of wolves hunts down a herd of deer. The feeding activity is often so intense that it may attract feeding birds which circle above, occasionally swooping down to pick up injured shad. Be alert for splashing activity on the surface during the summer and early fall, especially when accompanied by birds circling overhead. Acres of bass have been reported at such times. Typically, the fish aren't of lunker size, although we have seen 10-pounders schooling on top — a sight not soon forgotten! Schooling fish will attack almost any lure thrown into their midst with savage aggression, especially chrome topwater plugs or vibrating lures such as the Rat-L-Trap or Gay Blade. At other times, no lure can tempt them for some mysterious reason; these are the times to cast lures that will sink below the school of baitfish. A jigging spoon works beautifully here, cast it out and skip it across the surface 6 to 10 feet with the rod held high, then stop reeling suddenly and let the spoon tumble toward the bottom. The bass will usually nail it after it sinks a few feet. It is often fruitless to try to chase down the ever-emerging and disappearing schools of bass; better judgment would dictate maintaining a fixed position with your boat and using lures that can be cast a great distance, such as a spoon. During schooling activity, it's very common to hook two bass on one cast, so intense is their feeding. Remember that schooling bass represent a highly specialized feeding situation — the bass are after minnows or shad, not frogs or crayfish. A lure that approximates the general size, shape, and (especially) flash of the baitfish is to be selected for maximum productivity.

INFLOWING CREEKS – Bass often station themselves where muddy water meets clear water. Bass angler Alvin Burt from Brentwood, Tennessee, casts a spinnerbait into the murky reservoir.

Photo by Don Wirth

Inflowing Creeks

Creeks flowing into a reservoir, lake or river represent a change in the surrounding conditions, and, as we have seen, bass gravitate to anything different in their surroundings. In the hot summer months, bass will be attracted to an inflowing creek because the water there will most likely be cooler and more highly oxygenated. A small, tree-shaded creek is less likely to warm up as fast as a wide expanse of water typical of a lake or large river. Runoff after rainfall carries silt, mud, and sediment into the lake . . . and food such as worms, crayfish, etc. Fish will tend to station themselves at the edge of this changing water environment. The place where clear water meets murky water is often a prime bassin' spot, as the fish merely have to rush out and grab food as it flows by. A grub (soft plastic trailer on a jighead) crayfish-colored crankbait, or spinnerbait should catch bass in this situation.

Warm-Water Power Plant Discharges

The areas below power dams are most productive during the winter months when the lake or river water has cooled to the point where bass are very inactive. Often the water emerging from the turbines has been heated to the 90- or 100-degree range; as it reaches the colder water, it quickly cools to a temperature range that could spell great activity to the bass. *Seek out 72- to 82-degree water in these areas* and fish this water intently using structure spoons, large crankbaits, or the Do Nothing worm rig. Always be aware of safety when fishing during power generation — wear a life jacket at all times, not just when operating the big engine of your boat. Many other types of fish may also be caught in these conditions, including white bass, saltwater stripers, hybrids, sauger, walleye, catfish, gar, even paddlefish! It can be extremely productive and exciting winter fishing, perhaps the only fishing you'll be able to do in your area when the water cools drastically.

Rising Water

Rising water inundates many new areas in a lake or river, covering up new weeds, grass, brush, and bottom, and causing most of the bait to gravitate toward the shoreline. Rising water is typically bad news in a river, because it causes too much current. But in a lake it can provide great bassin' potential. A spinnerbait is the ideal lure to use when you've worked your way back into the deepest recesses of a newly flooded area. Author Wirth recalls a bass tournament he fished at Millwood Reservoir in Arkansas during the late fall in the early seventies. The water rose 25 ft. in the lake just prior to the tournament, inundating vast areas of forests, pastureland, and other varied terrain. One hundred twenty participants caught over one ton of bass in two days, many fish over 7 lbs. were taken and it took a 9-15 to win the big bass award! Participants reported fishing areas where No Trespassing signs were 3 ft. below the boat and bird nests (the real thing, not the baitcasting kind) were observed in bushes far below the surface!

Falling Water

When the water is falling, fish tend to move farther upstream . . . and so should you! All of the creatures living along the shoreline "pick up and move" from their normal cover and seek deeper holding stations. Any time there is a general, widespread movement of life in a body of water, you will find predators — bass included — moving in to take advantage of the situation. Crankbaits, jigs, and worms will all take bass when the water is falling.

New and Full Moon

There is a marked correlation between moon phase and activity of lower life forms, including bass. This is because many lower life forms utilize the new and full moon as a "clock" by which to time their spawning activities. As we know, bass spawn only once a year, and they definitely time their spawn to the new or full moon. But bass feed all through the year, and they become more active when minnows, insects, etc., are hatching out in droves. These hatches are attuned to the new or full moon. If these creatures hatched out a little at a time, they would soon be devoured by their predators. By timing their hatches and spawns at once, however, millions of young emerge and the perpetuation of the species is guaranteed, for no predator could possibly devour every hatching bass or minnow or insect . . . some are bound to survive! This is why lower life forms such as insects, fish, and amphibians lay great quantities of eggs and hatch huge numbers of young. They "know" that most will be eaten, but some will survive. While daily moon periods ("major" and "minor") should always be observed, *the new and full moon provide dramatic feeding opportunities for the bass, and the finest angling opportunities for the fisherman.* No special tips or techniques are necessary during these times — simply be on the water, fishing as you normally would. Your chances for success are far greater during these periods of lunar activity than at any other times during the month. When planning a special fishing trip, always try to center your activities around the full or new moon and your time and money investment in the trip is more likely to be rewarded. Doug Hannon's Moon Clock, a device for deter-

A double hit during a schooling bass "golden opportunity." Here Sports
Afield *editor Homer Circle and author Doug Hannon each tangle with a*

mining the best fishing days and time according to the lunar cycle, provides this lunar information in a compact form (see listing under "Miscellaneous Equipment" in the Appendix of this book).

The effect of the moon is too well documented for any fisherman to ignore. Before you head out, know when they'll be biting by checking the moon phase.

A simple handy reference like the MOON CLOCK shown here shows the best activity periods of the day and best days of the month to fish.

Power Generation in Reservoirs

In a reservoir, when power is generated, current is created. Even though the current may not be as noticeable in a lake as in a river, it pays to be on the lookout for telltale signs that they're "pulling water," as they say in the big lakes down South. Look for current pulling channel marker buoys forward as a sure sign that power is being generated. The movement of water in a big reservoir creates a spark of excitement in the chain of life existing there; small minnows will begin feeding as plankton drifts by, larger fish such as bluegills will move in to feed on the small minnows, and the bass will be attracted to these predators in the ever-increasing cycle of predation. Fish will move quickly to reposition themselves to escape from the current and to take advantage of food drifting by. Too much power generation, of course, can spoil the fishing, but a moderate amount will create great angling potential. In a huge reservoir the current will dissipate as it travels down the lake, because the lake usually gets wider toward the dam. In general, locate mounds, humps, and high spots such as sandbars or gravel shoals; bass will move up on top of these to prey on forage. Also concentrate on the narrowest parts of the lake where the effect of the current is maximized. Fish lures with a minimum of resistance for maximum productivity such as the jigging spoon, plastic worm, or Do Nothing rig; heavier sinkers may be necessary when using a worm rig to get the lure to the bottom. Large crankbaits such as the Maxi-R are very effective when fished over ledges and other structure in calmer areas out of the direct flow of the current where big bass might be holding. All feeding activity in a tailrace is often dependent upon the whims of the power company, and it pays to be apprised of generating schedules. This information is usually available through the TVA or Corps of Engineers' office at the dam.

Keeping Golden Opportunities in Perspective

Obviously, even the expert angler won't find these golden opportunities every day. When you find them, enjoy the tremendous bass fishing potential they offer, but remember that there's plenty to be said for the solitude and reflective aspects of the times when bassin' isn't quite so hot and heavy. Also, remember to think about the conservation aspects of these special moments and avoid "meat fishing" for bass at these times. Viewed in the proper framework, these special times are the gravy that adds spice to the meat-and-potatoes bassin' you'll be participating in at most other times. Enjoy!

Author Don Wirth's son, grateful for having caught this 9 lb. bass, release it back into the world of the bass.

Conservation Ethic

THE ENLIGHTENED bass fisherman of today fishes not for the accumulation of a collection of mounted fish, nor for the approval of others, but for his own inward reasons: fun, excitement, the enjoyment of nature, the appreciation of a great sport fish. Today, many fishermen are realizing that slaughter and conquest are not necessary components for the enjoyment of the sport of bass fishing. There are fewer bass today than ever before, and they are subject to more fishing pressure from more knowledgeable anglers than at any time in the past. If bass fishing were easy, there would be no need for this book. But it's tough . . . and getting tougher. *That's why we must view the bass as a precious natural resource, a resource to be enjoyed but a resource that is diminishing.* It's up to the individual angler to determine whether or not he wants to release a fish or take the time to "baby" his catch to make sure it survives after release. The novice angler, excited at the prospects of one day catching a big bass, may find it hard to imagine releasing such a trophy. Yet more and more anglers are doing just that every day because they realize the importance of all bass, especially the big ones, to the perpetuation of the species . . . and the sport. Let's examine the different forces which come into play in the world of bass fishing today, forces which will help you determine your own personal bass fishing conservation ethic.

"The Good Ol' Days"

Back in "the good ol' days" bass were so plentiful anyone could catch them. Thousands of huge bass were taken from prime fishing waters such as Florida's crystal-clear rivers by men and women who were totally unaware of the tremendous dent they would make in the bass fishery. "Green trout," as the largemouth bass used to be called, were taken on cane poles and heavy braided line, using live shiners or homemade lures. The numbers of fish caught were so vast, it seems impossible today; we would surely disbelieve it, save for the photographic evidence left behind.

Insurance agent Ray Scott (left) from Montgomery, Alabama, whose Bass Anglers Sportsman Society helped create the "bass boom" of the early seventies, is pictured with Bobby Murray on the winner's stand at the first B.A.S.S. Classic.

B.A.S.S. photo

The Bass Boom of the Seventies

The early seventies experienced the so-called "bass boom" when bass fishing gained widespread popularity by leaps and bounds. Perhaps no one was more responsible for this phenomenon than Montgomery, Alabama, insurance agent Ray Scott, who formed the Bass Anglers Sportsmen Society (B.A.S.S.) from a handful of names in a cigar box. Today, B.A.S.S. numbers over 450,000 members and represents a powerful economic — even political — force. Its publication, *Bassmaster* Magazine, covers the world of bass fishing and is the prestige publication of the sport. With the growth of organized fishing societies came competitive fishing — bass tournaments. While Ray Scott does not claim to be the inventor of bass tournaments, he certainly is the primary force behind their widespread popularity. Coinciding with the growth of tournaments was the growth of fishing clubs on the local level and the increasing popularity of bass boats, specialized fishing machines equipped with electronic gear.

With competitive fishing, new factors came into play. Many were no longer catching bass for the sheer enjoyment of it but rather to win money and prizes and to impress others with a heavy stringer. Organized fishing soon began to put a serious dent in the bass fishery, and organizations such as B.A.S.S. realized that the future of the sport lay in "catch and release." Most bass clubs and tournament organizers jumped on this bandwagon, and extra tournament points were given for fish weighed in alive, adding to the incentive.

Delayed Mortality

There seemed to be little criticism that could be leveled against fishermen who caught and released bass, yet studies in the late seventies and early eighties began to show a serious problem: delayed mortality. The fish were being released alive, yet many would die a few hours or days later. Today, concerned fishermen and major bass fishing organizations such as B.A.S.S. and Team Hydra-Sports require the use of chemical treatments in livewells and holding tanks to prevent shock and bacterial infestation. More articles are being written about the proper handling and "babying" of caught bass than ever before. Many bass guides permit only one trophy bass per client, with the rest to be released. The bass fishing public is getting more in tune with the times, and the dead-fish pictures in magazines are getting fewer and fewer.

A typical tournament weigh-in of the early seventies: stringers of dead meat. Today, a more enlightened approach prevails and not only are tournament bass usually released, livewells are treated with Jungle Laboratory's "Catch & Release" potion to help prevent delayed mortality.

Photo by Bob Bragg

The Government's View of Bass

Unfortunately, much of the perspective of bass anglers comes from the views of the various game and fish agencies of the U S. and state governments. These views are beginning to change in some states, in favor of more enlightened legislation. But in a bureaucracy change takes time; unfortunately, where the bass are concerned, time is rapidly running out. The following governmental viewpoints should be carefully scrutinized:

Limits are restrictions put on the number of fish, including bass, that may be taken in a given state or body of water. While at first glance they seem like a good idea, limits have a serious negative effect. Many fishermen think that they are not good enough unless they catch and take home their limit every time they go fishing. Thus, someone who started bass fishing for the sheer enjoyment of it may believe he is not much of a fisherman unless he kills ten bass or whatever the limit in his area may be. Many fishermen would be happy if the limit were one bass. The point is, don't let a government agency dictate what's a good and a bad fisherman. If you're happy catching two bass, so be it. Don't feel inadequate because you didn't catch ten fish.

Harvesting is the term used by government agencies to define the process of taking bass and other fish from our waterways by rod and reel. This concept views bass fishermen as farmers and bass as a crop, in effect. As a result, both the fish and the fisherman are demeaned. It's hard to think of a "crop" like soybeans and wheat as a living, moving creature. . . . Yet that's what the bass is — a living creature. Government agencies view it as favorable behavior to "harvest" a limit of bass; you don't return "soybean bass" to the lake. Think of the bass as a living thing, not as a crop; you'll appreciate the species and enjoy the sport much more.

Studies are constantly performed by government agencies and the college community on the sport fishery. Many of these seek to demonstrate the effects of industrial pollution, channelization, removal of habitat, etc. Knowledge is helpful, yet many of these studies are made for the sole purpose of perpetuating more studies. A study that says a lake is now dead because of industrial pollution is of little benefit; one that demonstrates pollution's presence in its earliest stages and seeks to find ways to stop it is of far greater import. Learn who your elected officials are — if your local fishing grounds are being ruined by industry, the advancement of civilization into previously unsettled areas or worse, tell him or her you're upset about it and ask what you can do to help stop it. Above all, demand that a larger portion of your fishing license dollars be spent in active programs which *solve* problems, not simply study them. If the results of a study are not implemented, that study is a waste of time and money.

Bass Clubs

Perhaps one of the fastest ways to gain knowledge about the sport of bass fishing, and especially about your local waters, is to join a bass club. Spending one day on the water with a knowledgeable angler willing to share what he knows will help put information gathered from other sources into a cohesive pattern. Suddenly the pieces of the puzzle will begin to fit! Choose a bass club interested in the catch and release of fish. Attend a club meeting and monitor what goes on. Is it a free-for-all or are the officers well organized? Is there something else going on besides tournaments planning? Is there any discussion of community service projects such as litter clean-up? Is it a club that gives something back to the community . . . and to the sport?

Trophy Bass

One day, hopefully, you will experience the incomparable thrill of having a lunker bass on the end of your line. We hope so! There's nothing wrong with wanting to mount that fish once you land it . . . *provided* it's mounted in the right spirit! Mount a bass to commemorate a special trip or as a symbol for your love of a great sport . . . *not* because it's over 5 or 6 or 10 lbs.! Avoid setting "plateaus" to conquer. Many anglers mount everything they catch over 5 lbs. In our view, this makes each successive trophy less significant. There is something sad these days about the angler with a wall full of mounted big bass . . . sad because of the enormous dent he put in the big fish population, and sad because he has demeaned the fish, himself, and the sport. Multiple trophies lose their individual significance. Fishing, as opposed to hunting, presents a rare opportunity . . . one can capture the prey *and* release it unharmed, thereby doubling his sense of fulfillment.

Formulate Your Own Conservation Ethic

Ultimately, whether or not you choose to release a bass is totally up to you. However, we do urge that you ask yourself what *you* want to do, instead of relying on competitive pressure, the need to impress others, or fallacious reasoning by government bureaucracies to make up your mind for you. Bass fishing is what *you* make it. Will you make it something truly special?

Appendix

Because of the tremendous variety of bass fishing lures, rods, reels and related equipment — much of it similar in nature — we have attempted to list equipment that has performed favorably for us. There are, of course, many others who are also reliable. The following Appendix should assist the bass fisherman in locating the equipment, publications and organizations specifically mentioned in this book; addresses of manufacturers are included for those products which are mail order or hard to find. All others should be at your local tackle shops.

HOOKS, LINES, AND TERMINAL TACKLE:

Hooks: Mustad hooks (O. Mustad & Sons [U.S.A.] Inc.);
Tru-Turn hooks (Tru-Turn, Inc.)

Line: Maxima line (Bruce B. Mises, Inc.); Stren line (Du Pont Corp.); Trilene line, Cros-Lok swivels (Berkely and Company).

RODS AND REELS:

Ambassadeur and Cardinal reels (ABU-Garcia).
Daiwa rods and reels (Daiwa Corporation).
Fenwick rods (Fenwick/Woodstream Corporation).
Slider rods (Slider Company, 511 East Gaines Street, Lawrenceburg, TN 38464) — (615) 762-4700.
Shimano rods and reels (Shimano American Corporation).
Zebco rods and reels (Zebco Division, Brunswick Corporation).
CUSTOM RODS including Roberts wrap:
Rev. Bill Conine, 2005 Rose Avenue, Americus, GA 31709 — (912) 924-0684.
Bill Poe, P.O. Box 43, Staley, NC 27355 — (803) 622-2622.

LURES:

Hula Popper, Jitterbug: Fred Arbogast Company, 313 West North St., Akron, OH 44303 — (216) 253-2177.
Balsa crankbaits and topwater plugs: Jim Bagley Bait Company, P.O. Box 110, Winter Haven, FL 33880 — (813) 294-4271.
Super Vibrax spinners, Floyd's Buzzer: Blue Fox Tackle Company, 645 North Emerson, Cambridge, MN 55008 — (612) 338-6695.
Bomber, Model A, Bushwacker: Bomber Bait Company, P.O. Box 1058, Gainesville, TX 76240 — (817) 655-5505.
WeedBeater soft plugs: Burke Fishing Lures, 1969 South Airport Road, Traverse City, MI 49684 — (616) 947-5010.
Do Nothing Worm, Jack's Jigging Spoon: Jack Chancellor Lure Company, P.O. Box 1608, Phenix City, AL 36867.
Big O, Hot Spot: Cordell Tackle, Inc., 3601 Jenny Lind, Fort Smith, AR 72902 — (501) 782-1607.
Scoundrel Plastic worms: Creme Lure Company, P.O. Box 87, Tyler, TX 75710 — (214) 593-7371.
Dardevle spoons: Eppinger Manufacturing Company, 6340 Schaefer Highway, Dearborn, MI 48126 — (313) 582-3205.

LURES:

Bill Plummer's Super Frog: Harrison Hoge Industries Inc., Department Ba43L, St. James, NY 11780.

Tiny Torpedo, Lucky 13, Zara Spook: James Heddon's Sons, 414 West Street, Dowagiac, MI 49047 — (616) 782-5123.

Hopkins spoons: Hopkins Fishing Lures, Inc., 1130 Boissevain Avenue, Norfolk, VA 23507 — (804) 622-0977.

Krocodile spoons: Luhr Jensen & Sons, Inc., P.O. Box 297, Hood River, OR 97031 — (800) 547-2320.

Johnson Silver Minnow: Johnson Fishing, Inc., 1531 Madison Avenue, Mankato, MN 56001 — (507) 345-4623.

Mirrolure: L & S Bait Company, Inc., 1500 East Bay Drive, Largo, FL 33541 — (813) 584-7691.

Rat-L-Trap: Bill Lewis Lures, P.O. Box 4062, Alexandria, AL 36027 — (205) 687-5716.

Jelly Worms, Top Cat, Finn Mann: Mann's Bait Company, P.O. Box 604, Eufaula, AL 36027 — (205) 687-5716.

Sassy Shad, plastic trailers: Mister Twister, Inc., P.O. Drawer 996, Minden, LA 71055 — (318) 377-8818.

Big N, Little N, other plugs: Norman Manufacturing Co., Highway 96 East, Greenwood, AR 72936 — (501) 996-2125.

Rapala lures: Normark Corporation, 1710 East 78th Street, Minneapolis, MN 55423 — (612) 869-3292.

Whistler: Northland Tackle Company, Route 4, Box 71, Bemidji, MN 56601 — (218) 751-6723.

Big Mousie and Little Mousie: Petey MacLure Co., P.O. Box 2321, 9509 Beach Circle, Inverness, FL 32650 — (904) 344-8321.

Rebel, Deep Wee R, Maxi R: Plastics Research & Development Co., 3601 Jenny Lind, Fort Smith, AR 72902 — (501) 782-8971.

Red Eye lures: Red Eye Lures, Inc., 6619 Oak Orchard Road, Elba, NY 14058 — (716) 757-9958.

Mepps spinners: Sheldon's Inc., 626 Center Street, Antigo, WI 54409 — (715) 623-2382.

Slider lures: Slider Company (see listing under "Rods & Reels").

Devil's Horse: Smithwick Lures, Inc., P.O. Box 1205, Shreveport, LA 77163 — (318) 929-2318.

Uncle Josh pork rinds, Pedigo Spinrite: Uncle Josh Bait Company, 524 Clarence Street, Fort Atkinson, WI 53538 — (414) 563-2491.

Hellbender, Dirty Bird: Whopper Stopper Inc., P.O. Box 1111, Sherman, TX 75090 — (214) 893-6557.

Rooster Tail: Worden's Lures, P.O. Box 310; Granger, WA 98932 — (509) 854-1311.

Booza Bug and Booza Fly jigs, Aggravator: Zorro Bait Company, Route 6, Box 139C-3, Sparta, TN 38583 — (615) 761-2295.

MARINE ELECTRONICS

Depth finders, video and chart recorders, surface temperature meters: Lowrance Electronics; Techsonic Industries, Inc.; and Vexilar.
Loran C: SI-TEX Marine Electronics, Inc.

BOATS & ACCESSORIES

Aluminum bass boats: Bass Pro Shops; Dura Craft; and Fisher Marine.
Fiberglass bass boats: Cajun; Champion; Hydra-Sports, Ranger; and Skeeter.
Outboard motors: Mariner; Mercury; OMC; and Yamaha.
Weedless trolling motors: Motor-Guide.

MISCELLANEOUS EQUIPMENT

Catalog mail order, complete line of fishing tackle and accessories: Bass Pro Shops, P.O. Box 4046, Springfield, MO 65807 — (800) 227-7776.
Cabela's, 812-13th Avenue, Sidney, NE 69160 — (800) 237-4444.
Catch and Release livewell compound: Jungle Labs, Box 630, Cibolo, TX 78108 — (800) 327-2200.
Mail Order, Hannon's MOON CLOCK, Books and MULE Anchor: Tern Corporation, P.O. Box 3123, Seminole, FL 33542 — (813) 392-8842.

ORGANIZATIONS AND PUBLICATIONS

Bass Anglers Sportsman Society, 1 Bell Road, Montgomery, AL 36141 — (205) 272-9530.
Bass Research Foundation, P.O. Box 99, Starkville, MS 39759 — (601) 323-3131.
In Fisherman Magazine, R.R. 8, Box 999, Brainerd, MN 56401 — (218) 829-1648.
International Game Fish Association (IFGA), 3000 East Las Olas Blvd., Fort Lauderdale, FL 33316 — (305) 467-0161.
Pro Bass Magazine, 15115 South 76th East Avenue, Bixby, OK 74008 — (918) 366-4441.
Rooster Tales Magazine, Team Hydra-Sports, 526 East Iris Drive, Nashville, TN 37204 — (615) 385-2221.

RECOMMENDED BOOKS

The Bass Boat Bible, by Earl Bentz and Don Wirth, B & W Publishing Co., c/o Stratos Boats, 931 Industrial Road, Old Hickory, TN 37138.
Bass Fishing Fundamentals, by Ken Schultz, World Angling Services, RD 1, Box 52-Y, Forestburgh, NY 12701 — (914) 794-3941.
Hannon's Field Guide for Bass Fishing, by Doug Hannon and W. Horace Carter, Tern Corporation (see listing under "Miscellaneous Equip.")

More Great Outdoors

HOW TO FISH FOR SNOOK: By Earl Downey. Snook fishing is one of Florida's most popular outdoor sports. Tips on locations, methods, bait, tackle — how to handle a strike — and more, give fishermen an edge on catching the wary snook. Cleaning methods and recipes included. Illustrated with line drawings; 64 pages.
Soft cover $2.95

GUNKHOLER'S CRUISING GUIDE TO FLORIDA'S WEST COAST. By Tom Lenfestey. New expanded edition now covers the coast from the Everglades to the Alabama state line, with an added bonus of two rivers — the Suwannee and the Apalachicola — and the Okeechobee Waterway from Ft. Myers to the Atlantic via Lake Okeechobee. Local information not on your charts. Where to find anchorages, fuel, ice, food, repair centers. If you sail in these areas, you need this book aboard. New Edition, Dec. 1st, 1986. Size 8½x11. Soft Cover $9.95

MAKE & MEND CAST NETS: By Ted Dahlem. The only complete book of cast nets — covering the use of monofilament and nylon in making cast nets. Diagrams and illustrations included to show you how to make, repair and use your cast net. Size 5½x8½, 72 pages.
Soft Cover. $2.95

DICTIONARY OF FISHES: By Rube Allyn. Widely acclaimed identification book. World records; food value; habits and habitats — over 700 illustrations, many in color. Size 8½x11; 140 pages.
Soft cover $5.95

FLORIDA FISHES: By Rube Allyn. This tackle-box size book will help you identify the most common fish found in Florida waters. Get a copy for yourself and one for a visiting fisherman from "the north". 80 pages. Size 5½x8½.
Soft Cover $2.95

LAUNCHING AND CRUISING GUIDE FOR MID-FLORIDA. By Ernie B. Miller. If you have a boat you launch from a trailer, you need this book. Shows you where to find the launching ramps, and what to expect to find when you reach them — fees, parking, facilities, etc. Includes 26 charts on Florida's lakes, rivers, and coastal waters. Size 8½x11, 72 pages.
Soft Cover $5.95

HOW TO COOK YOUR CATCH: By Rube Allyn. Now that you've caught it, how do you cook it? This book gives you a variety of recipes for each of 22 kinds of the fish you bring home. Also included are illustrated instructions for cleaning your catch. Size 5¼x8½, 80 pages.
Soft Cover $1.95